Hummadruz

For my family and friends

And I have discovered bee-swarms in the earth:
I've heard them when I lie in the June grass
on hot still days, humming under my head,

under my hands, down in the earth's hive —
or is the world buzzing?

Hummadruz

Hilary Llewellyn-Williams

seren

seren

is the book imprint of
Poetry Wales Press Ltd
Nolton Street, Bridgend, Wales
www.seren-books.com

ISBN 1-85411-306-2

A CIP record for this title is available from
the British Library.

*The publisher works with the financial assistance
of the Arts Council of Wales.*

Cover photograph by Sian Parker

Printed in palatino by Bell & Bain Ltd, Glasgow

Contents

The Tree Calendar (1987)

Book of Shadows (1990)

The Tree Calendar

Mole

A labourer, her body is her tool
warm velvet spade in the cold ground;
blind snout, the enemy of worms,
she tunnels like a gang, chucking up soil.

Little miner, her glossy coat made soft breeches
a patchwork coat smelling of earth after rain:
fit wear for a chilly chapel Sunday,
a windy burial, a son's birth.

Black hermit, toiling alone in the dark
her body shifts with the unseen year:
when its season is past she closes the eye of her sex
becomes neuter, mechanical rooter.

Dodger of two-footed death and the cat's fangs
she presides in a fortress of roots and stones;
calmly ploughing about her own business
she sinks her shafts, subverting our foundations.

Stone Study

(Barbara Hepworth's carving studio, St Ives, Cornwall)

High light from a sky-window
sea-facing north, the best of sun
for shaping, as artists know,

patterns this room to a sculpted
stillness, that was all noise
and movement: voices fretted

the three-dimensional clear air,
ringing of chisels, slap of clay,
heaving, jostling of that block there

into place, the creaking wide
of the tall bolted double door
for big deliveries, the bite

of metal into stone. And at
its dusty hub, a busy woman:
who is absent now. She left

her overalls and jackets hung
on nails, stained with age and plaster;
a rag in one pocket, a hammer slung

in another. Sea-reflected
warm light poses a cold stone
for one more blow, always deflected.

So a white slab waits in her place
feathered with frost-strokes, rippling
delicate skin on every face

and a muscular swell beneath.
There's a fat brooding shape
emerging from the block in low relief

immeasurably ancient, head
slightly inclined in the old way,
hinting at life down in the dead

rock under us. And the sculpture's
done, perfect; roundly tuned
to its own rough echoes. The rock stirs.

Crossing Bridges

Keep moving, and don't look down.
Just a thin skin of stretched
metal, or wood, or stone
divides the abyss over which
you travel. Something risky,
unreachable, lies below;
and beyond, the next place

which is your destination
from this end of the bridge
barely glimpsed, like the future.
You are nowhere, simply spanning
a space between worlds, between earth
and earth, while beneath
you the water slides and pulls

or traffic hurtles into oblivion.
High winds on the Severn Bridge sway
thirty-ton lorries: the masses creak
and crack: the river's a long
way down. And yet in Tibet they
thread ropes across chasms, one
for your feet and one at each shoulder

in case you need to hold on;
throw logs across boiling torrents,
cross death at a run with packs
on their backs, weave bridges
to dip and swing between mountains, safe
where we'd sweat and slip, they keep
moving, and don't look down.

The Tree Calendar

"Make an effort to remember. Or failing that, invent."
(*Monique Wittig* — *Les Guérrillères*)

This is a cycle of poems based on an ancient Celtic 13-month calendar. There are various versions of the calendar, including an early Welsh one, but I have used the older Gaelic version known as the Beth-Luis-Nion, as it is less complicated and more widely known.

Each 28-day month is named after a tree, which has its particular place in the year due to symbolic and magical associations. The tree names are also the names of letters in the Gaelic alphabet. In its original form, the Gaelic alphabet had thirteen consonants, and these were given the names of the thirteen calendar trees. This is an example of the widespread ancient belief that trees and language (especially writing) were mystically linked. I am reaffirming this link through these poems.

My source for the Beth-Luis-Nion calendar was *The White Goddess* by Robert Graves. Graves, through a combination of scholarship and creative imagination, connected the trees, and their symbolism, with the seasonal cycles, myth and poetry. He was convinced that he'd stumbled upon a coded key to the mysteries of prehistoric religious belief. Whatever the truth of that, I and many others have been stimulated by the images of the Beth-Luis-Nion. These poems are my attempt to explore further possibilities by relating some of these images to my own experience, during the course of a year (1985). As the year drew to a close and I completed the last poem, Robert Graves died, thus bringing the whole sequence round to completion.

In case anyone is wondering what happens to the 365th day in the (solar) year, that extra day (23rd December) has no month. It does have a tree, the Yew, one of the five 'vowel' trees, but for reasons of symmetry I left it out of the cycle.

15

Birch/*Beth*
December 24 — January 20

After Twelfth Night comes the reality
of winter. When the greenery's stripped down
it's barefaced, blowing under the door.
Mean days dragging out a fraction more
before dark, make our myth of spring
ridiculous. I walk out into the stark
endless moment of January.

Old snow slumps in the hedge,
stretching the fields
wet to the birchwood, raw
black tangle against the grey.
Mud ruts, brown ice under my boot
snaps and seeps as I trudge up
to the sad ranks of trees, the thin
skin birches in their thaw.

These brittle twigs swept clear of leaves
whipping along the light,
points of dark bud concealing green,
I'll tie a bundle to my broom, for flight:
no shelter here, the rain falls through
this frostwood, the sky stares between.
The bramble jags, the stag horns of the scrub
bad musk of leafmould, in the dusk
that stirs behind my shoulder.

Birch stems lean to the loud stream
crowding beneath the wind,
thrashing their rods at winter stumps,
at the cracked, dimwit days.
Think of the woods brushed with a green haze.

Think of the covered hills
filling with cleaner light, and a gap
in the clouds for something to glance through.
I stoop in a cold shade
gathering twigs for a journey.

Rowan/*Luis*
January 21— February 17

Bride put her finger in the river
on the feast day of Bride,
and away went the hatching-mother of the cold.
                              (Gaelic Prayer)

The roaring is loud and brown.
I hold water in the cup of my hand
it warms to my touch like blood

but I dare not put my feet to the flood:
I would be swept in the coils
of serpents and rolled to the sea.

Rain blows its feathers around me:
it tickles my face, quickens my skin.
Here is where I came down

this steep bank from a dark town
full of winter, to find the world
at a turning point. And here

I climb upwards from the sheer
rainwet drop, and I'm full of moon
and movement. Cautiously

I rest my fingers on a rowan tree
for a wand and a brand to avert
evil, a tree that's spun

Full of fire, with the swelling sun
in its stubby black bud
and I've broken a twig clean;

inside it is sweet and green,
promising bundles, clusters of red.
A word said: and a bird flown.

18

Ash/*Nion*
February 18 — March 17

Why is the ash the tree of quickening,
this month of green spikes with an early sun
shining straight in our eyes? What has it got
to do with bird's wings or the snowdrop's spark?

Its blunt shut buds are stubborn: not a crack
open, though the willow's tipped with silk;
it stays the same dull grey from the first day
of Lent till the first of May, while the earth

turns green around it. Ash is a strange tree,
coloured like cold water, and inside
sea-grained, close-rippled; but it burns
hot, fresh or dry. The bark so thin

and fine as skin, reminding me of horses.
All ash-lore, ash-mythologies run through
my brain in twisted threads. A wizard god
hung from his heels like some marauding crow

hoping to fill his brilliant emptiness
with consciousness, with webs of poetry.
Since then, we've lost our art of memory,
dismembered like the god. So I must go

to try that ancient weird hypothesis:
to learn the source of summer from the tree
in my own garden; which seems stark and still,
until I slide my hands down its smooth flank

and feel it shiver. In the encircled heart
something vibrates from skin to skin — and how
those blackstopped boughs curve upwards into blue,
fingering the invisible stars of spring!

The tremor travels down a million stones
to the muffled pulse of water. As all worlds
are tangled in its branches, so are we,
linked by the fibre fluids of the tree.

Ash breathes beneath my hands; it's full of tension,
ready to bound away with our next gale,
galloping in the hedge. And at its foot
something spins webs. I have remembered now.

Alder/*Fearn*
March 18 — April 14

Bwlchwernen: the alder pass.
The world swoops west
tilts valley and hill,
to the sudden light of spring,
the long, brushed shadows.

Water shines from the fields.
A brimful river sweeps
roots of alder, leaving
the rolled corpse of a lamb
to bob in the shallows.

Up here, in a stone barn
this Easter, a straggle
of children and adults saw
the outlawed story retold
of an old resurrection:

a grain reborn as a child
(as we sat in the straw):
a lost child fostered and found
to be wizard of poets, a star
with the wind's protection.

Out in the yard, our cars
mud-axled, we dispersed
turned away from the scene.
Now I visit my alder stream
in a double life, knowing

that nothing's been lost. A raven
croaks *Brân* overhead:
banished westward, but still
surviving. And alder flowers
green as thieves, still growing.

Willow/*Saille*
April 15 — May 12

One spring I came to an unlucky place.
I carried love in a bundle on my back
and I stepped over the brink of an adventure,
wide-open, foolish. The house was dark
and nervous; the ground around
was full of willows. Their poison entered me
like swallowed water, easily.

They leaned, pollarded knobs along the streams
with witches' raised hair.
They thickened the air with something invisible:
the clay, too, was clogged with it.
Their long-flint leaves rubbed quietly
together. All the way to the edge
of the sky stood dead elms, bleached
to bone, like a winter landscape.

The corpse elms leached their deaths into the soil
and the willows bloated
drawing pain like a poultice, sucking grief
from abandoned farms and a spoilt, lumpy land
awaiting an expansion of the town
with new roads leading nowhere.
There I felt cursed: my head swum
in the sunken garden, and my energies
trickled into the mud. Mosquitoes swarmed.

Now I can love willows again, in a wild
country. Their silver softens the hedge:
their gold attracts early bees.
When I touch their stems, they tremble.
But in the wind they winnow secretly;
and I'm wary of a power that drags at me
as the moon drags the seas.

Hawthorn/*Huath*
May 13 — June 9

May's out: white, plump and plush
way-marker, sweet female unlucky spray;
tucked starry flowers, a million eyes
road-watching, field-guarding, a hilltop
presence, yearly more curved
with each twist of the earth, deep musk,
queen of long dusk, sharp secrets, she'll
turn to blood in the hedge, rich burning
drops. Jets leap and scream
through a damaged sky: my skin
darkens in so much light. The tightening
drum. The hum of silage cutters
from a far field, muffled by bushy May.
Smother those savage thorns
in green and white: she will be beautiful.
In a changed world, still she draws you,
enters you, as woman to woman;
and you are not hurt, but healed and washed
clean, even now, wise-eyed, reborn.

Oak/*Duir*
June 10 — July 7

I put my head in the bag of leaves
and breathed green. Coarse sourjuiced crushed
smell of wet summers, that sharp male taste;
foliate-faced I sucked green with each breath,
spaced out on oak. The fine drenching rain
felt seasidey. We walked the gleaming lane
that ribbons from hill to hill, slowly, dodging
odd Sunday cars, to our knees in tangled stalks,
flowering grasses, red cloverheads weighed down
with so much wet, the ditches murmuring.

Wine from oakleaves is tawny, tastes dark
and woody, midsummer evening fires, the sweet
smoke of peat. It is strong, climbs down deep
and blazes. It comes from the young growth;
the tender pink-flushed clusters of new leaf
offer themselves at a touch, break free
in showers of droplets, stalked green and sapped
like frankincense. You pour boiling water
on the stripped leaves: they smell of fresh tea.
The brew is bitter and brown; it could cure leather.

I sipped at last year's wine; thought, from now on
the nights draw in. The season's prime lay
stewed in a bin, filling our house with summer.
(I'm autumnal, best in receding light
in the dark half of the year.) Next day
I strained the stuff, added yeast and sweetness,
set the warm juice to work. Those clear green leaves
are bloodless now, bleached out: I have
their essence bottled up, breathed in, elixir of all
oaks in me, as the sun inches south.

Holly/*Tinne*
July 8 — August 4

Here in high summer, holly sets fruit
that will redden come Christmas.
Its prickles gloss and crackle in the sun.
Those deathless leaves make holly king.

This tree is holy, but not kind. What
is this holiness? What gift of grace
is so sharp-edged, dark-branched, hedged
with superstition, crowned with thorn?

Last summer's holly scratched my small
son as he climbed a bank, from rib
to breastbone a long stripe, with beads
of berry-blood, a flaxen Christ, arms up

and crying. This summer's rain
has blighted our best crops; but the trees
thrive, the trees take precedence. Green
under grey skies: reign of wood and water.

As the days shorten, holly's power grows:
ripening power, the birth power, power
from behind the eyes, dream power, spear-
leaved and bitter-barked and full of berries.

Holly saplings under graveyard yews
like prongs of resurrection, spring
from the shadows. The yews red-fleshed
and folded secretly, gave birth to them.

Blood mixed with soil was the old way
harvests grew fat, and holly ruled the feast.
My torn child heals: a ragged silver line
across his breast, fades as he flourishes.

Hazel/*Coll*
August 5 — September 1

After last night's rain
light gathers on hazel leaves
with their three-clumped nuts,
and a wide-angled sun
shapes precise hills and stones.

I drag my hand through water.
Cresses stroke my skin,
which shrinks from their fleshiness.
I cup, and scoop to drink
what runs through my fingers.

A cold, sweet-metal taste:
water reflected on stone.
Myself reflected in water
shadowed and blurred, a dark
disturbance within the pool.

Tendrils of water spill down
inside me, tracing cool paths.
I splash my forehead and lids,
and wish for knowledge, for solid
sense, for a way through.

Knowledge and clarity
I need so much; I've let so
much slip by. In a hidden place
there's a well with my face in it
smudged silver, flickering,

and hazels growing thick
overhead: and there
my eyes look out from depths
of past and future, watching
the hazel ripples lift and spread.

Bramble/Vine/*Muin*
September 2 — September 29

The smell of heaped-up blackberries in a bowl:
I am caught, small, in a rough dusty lane
leading to pinewoods, to a shining lake,
and the burnt house on the hill.
Hot full September smell; years beyond years
polish the ripening woods to gold, to falls
of chestnuts by the school, clutches of sudden
mushrooms (Do Not Touch) and scarlet
hawthorn, evening fires, and blackberries.

The trouble we had to pick them! Scrambling
up banks and over fences, into rotting ditches,
stung, scratched, tousled, burred —
yet spurred on by the purple on our tongues
and promised heaps of sweetness.
We trampled secret ways to the best clumps
through willow-herb and nettles, crouched
in a den with arching thorny stems
above us, counting our store.
That powerful, smoky fragrance. Those big
ripe berries, soft with sour blood
I sucked from my reddened fingers.

Brambles and brambles, season after season
straggle and tangle, whip out new shoots
to flower and fruit. Each year
whole families desert their cars to look
at hedgerows and waste thickets, reach
into thorns for pleasure. The plain sight
of blackberries is irresistible. It wakes
our stone-age lust for scrounging, scrumping, till
we seem to be on nature's side again,
drawn in, intoxicated; while the dark
juices of memory ferment and rise
and I, by a ruined house, gather my treasure.

Ivy/*Gort*
September 30 — October 27

In the dawn fields, white fogs lie breathing,
　　making a Chinese landscape:
the Nine Kings of the North Pole descend.

Cattle shifting in the near distance
　　sidle away from winter;
step by step, it has surrounded them.

The trees look thinner in this long sun:
　　drawing their juices in, they
contemplate dark traceries of mould.

Brown and gold brushstrokes over the hills.
　　A smell of frost and woodfires;
ivy increasing as the leaves fall.

Flowering ivy for the late bees
　　full blown and glossy, tightens
its massive grip, defies the cold Kings,

keeping slow but certain purposes:
　　enveloping the whole world
in patterned mounds of vegetation.

Here is a ruined cottage, sprouting
　　leaves, snake-stemmed and rustling:
part of the woods now, splitting apart.

The roof gone, how can the structure stand?
　　Ivy has loosened its knots.
Stone by stone, it is undone again.

From a roost above the fallen hearth
　　an owl calls in full sunlight:
the Nine Kings of the North Pole descend.

But they step down from whatever heights
   they journeyed in, with keen joy,
trailing blue air, a ripened sun.

There is a large fruit, still uneaten.
   Look through a crack in the door.
Nine Kings treading ivy on the floor.

Reed/*Ngetal*
October 28 — November 24

A wind rises up
from the wetlands,
carries the cry of the sea
in deepening gusts to my door.
I draw in my head, snail
in a stone shell, doubtfully.

Southwest sunset
catches the trees, splays
out their shapes like spread
nerves, webbed and strung
vessels of drowsy fluid,
warming dull stalks to a richer
brown, until the wind
lifts heavy wings and all colours
flatten out. A long note
sounds in our chimney: winter's flute,

blowing from the throats
of reeds in the waste ground
down by the river. The dead
once fished there, dragged their nets,
crouched in the sedge for duck
and plover, stole eggs in spring.
They sheltered under reeds
in these sodden hills;
reed roofs and low stone walls
tucked down to earth,
shut in from the flapping light.

Our fenlands, wastes,
moors, marshes and wild sloughs
are shrunken now, ploughed up —
but give them time. Decay

puts out its tendrils. Water
seeps upwards patiently.
Stands of reeds sing
high from behind clenched teeth,
knot their roots tight,
bow to the seasons, keep firm
and yielding. Lost souls
glint from the shallows.

All night the gale
scuds over us. Dawn
will be more naked still:
the trees will be peeled sticks.
I close my eyes and pull
the covers up, but lie
aware of blind movements:
small shift of the house
downwards, the closing in
of winter, thread of roots
through water — and here's
that noise again, that shrill
dark reedy whistling.

Elder/*Ruis*
November 25 — December 22

Elder in its own season —
the old dregs of the year —
is utterly empty, surely the worst
tree in the hedge, stripped dead,
gnarled and twisted afflicted
sticks, like some crabbed arthritic
witch, pale driftwood blown
inland by the gale, to catch
grotesquely by its twigs: only force
of will can colour it now thick with fruit,
or remoter still, cream-flowered,
smelling of days past, days of promise, summer.

Tree of death of all trees,
all plants; elder from Hell,
that twilight country under the hill
or holy well, where Mother Holda shakes
her feather pillows out, and we have snow.
Elf-tree: avoid it after dark
and in the dark of the year, lurking
place of the Huldre-folk, who look fair
enough, but whose backs are hollow
as stumps, damp cavities; and still
they dance on the bare margin of our world.

This wine has all the weight
of fruit in it, weight of long days,
sticky and rich with iron, blood
sour with memory. It soothes my throat.
I picked those berries in another time
a sunlit day, with women
I no longer see. The elderberries hung

like grapes; their branches sagged,
snapped as we tugged them free, three
women under the green eye of the hill,
that massive mound built by the elder
tribe, the dark ones, thieves and dancers.

The world has tilted far
from the sun, from colour and juice.
I am tired. I draw myself in
from what's happening out there
in the rain's ragged shadows.
I am waiting for a birth
that will change everything: the earth
born over and over;
the cold eye of light slowly widening —
these hard buds guarding our unopened time.

*****

Old Mother, give me of thy wood:
and I shall give some of mine
what I turn into a tree

Letter to my Sister

It is summer where you are, but I am cold
as I write this, and my house is dark all day,
and the garden soaks up rain like a black sponge.
You will spend Christmas, you say,
trekking the mountain roads and the coast paths
with that giant man of yours. I picture you
lean and brown, frowning into the sun
shouldering your pack with the supple grace
I loved. I can see your face
clear as light, open as day: sunshine
is true to you. The flowers are strange
where you live, they speak Maori names
like the knock of wood on wood;
the birds crack words in your primeval trees.

I catch a dream of you; and here it is,
your blue note through my door. Pressed
in the thin folds like a paper flower
you wave to me, you sound your brand-new vowels
inflecting to the page-end, quick and small.
I look for more of you, and raise my eyes
to the far edge of the world. Down there,
beneath the roar of oceans, where the stars
make different shapes, where summer is,
lives someone that I knew in the cold wind
that blew along my shore. And as I turn
towards the sun, so she recedes
into the dark. My sister in the skin
circling with the earth, keep good your seasons.

Candlemas

On Brigid's Night
there was rain and wind and miles of darkness between us:
there was a generation of pain between us,
but I stayed awake for love's sake, and because of the candles.

On Brigid's Night
spring was calling a long way off, below the horizon
invisible, but heard, like a changed note:
my ears attuned, I lit candles around the room.

My children slept
upstairs, bundles of summer. I was tight-strung
and humming. Nineteen points of fire
in a small room needed watching; I sat with them.

My eyes half-closed
I watched them burn all night, watched wax spill pools
and curl and flow, the flames dip low,
wrapped round in shadows, caught in the eye of light.

The night you died
I talked to you through webs of sleep, recalling
you in my years of childhood
solid and sure, filling the fiery spaces.

I slept at last
towards dawn, in a darkened room. Slowly I woke
to sunlight striping the carpet, the cold
little heaps of wax: and my children shouting, and spring

one day nearer
and bottles clanking outside, and a sense of peace
and freedom; then the shrill cry
of the telephone, which I stumbled up to answer.

Stones

My garden grows stones.
I pluck them one by one
the flat grey, square buff, cobble pebbles;
but the rain brings them again.
Stones like weeds, like grain
shine in the wind that shrinks grass
with all my precious seedlings brought low:
on this gritty hill
growing nightlong, spitting soil
that I turn, turning up bones.

Breadmaking

Forgive the flour under my fingernails
the dabs of dough clinging to my skin:
I have been busy, breadmaking.
So easy, the flakes falling feathery
into the warm bowl, as I dip and measure
and pour the foaming treasured brown
yeast down to the ground wheat grain.
O as the barm breaks and scatters
under my working fingers like a scum
of tides on shifting sands, the secret cells
swell, you can smell their life
feeding and beating like blood
in my bunched palms
while I lift the lump and slap it back again.

It moves, like a morning mushroom,
a breathing side, stirring, uncurling
animal nudged from sleep; so I pummel
and thump and knuckle it into shape
to see it unwind like a spring
soft as a boneless baby on the table.
I have covered it now: let it grow
quietly, save for the least rustle
of multiplication in the damp bundle
telling of motion in the fattening seeds.
Its body's an uproar as I open the burning door —
it gives one final heave, and it blossoms out
to the brown loaf I have spread for you.
Taste the butter touching its heart like snow.

Watching Fulmars

(for Kate Johnson)

The path ends here, on the brink
of a drop, the sea in a thrash
below: sky ribbed and blue, sun pale

and interesting. Spring almost with us.
I am nervous at the cliff edge,
but must crane round to view

where fulmars nest on sheer black
battlements of rock, slip to and fro
plump bodies and spread wings

soundlessly turning and rising eye
to my eye, making me sway.
We can walk no more this way,

but must fall, or fly, or return
down the sparse earth track
we laboured up, and look

for new showing green, to justify
the double journey. You stand poised
as if for flight: huge silence watches you.

I still my mind's eternal chattering.
Where the words were, grey and white birds
open their wings, glide over on the wind.

The Gardener's Daughter

In the gloom of a dusty shed
    lay seed potatoes, rows of knobble faces
staring at me, exhaling a sharp reek
    of the underworld, stopping my breath with mould.
I'd sit with them, half-afraid,
    listening to the tinny noise of rain
and your voice from the outer world of the stone yard.

Your movements were large and slow,
    steady, skilful, lifting a laden barrow
with ease, in the long light of the afternoon;
    or in the sea-light of the glasshouses
you strung tomato trusses
    with their heavy, jungle smell,
and played the monsoon of the snaking hose.

My movements were quick and small
    making my feet ring on the iron floor
following you along the leafy rows
    plucking out weeds to please you.
Squat in my rubber boots I'd fill the pots
    shovelling compost with the narrow trowel
proudly wearing my work in my fingernails.

I held the slipping knots
    as we wound raffia round squeaking stems
of tulips, freesias, dahlias: but you
    carried the precious flowers in your huge hands
much gentler than mine, to the water.
    And I, the gardener's daughter
my face to the swimming blooms, conjuring rainbows.

From the East, Where the Sun Rises

Clear as an eye, lifted lid,
raised lid of earth, breaking shell,
bud breaking, unfolding,
slant golden blade, green blazing,
sun open wide, spring rising.

From the rim of the east
from the sun's house
a heron
follows his heart to the river
with slow, strong wings.
Eggs in the wet reeds,
the alder roots. On a hill
hares dance; on screaming swings
children fly up, laughing.

His wings beat for love
for the pool where his love waits.

The sun's level gaze, the brave
white-faced snowdrops
sharp in the dark under a hedge bank;
everywhere there are eyes, eyes.
Wings in the bare twigs, everywhere,

and green blazing golden blades
pushing and prodding, unfolding,
breaking and budding, pale flooding
pools in the dusk, black tips
swelling against the last
of the light, and dawn's first light
due east, in the sun's house.

Due east, heron and hare,
kids shouting, clouds running,
mud growing, snow on the hills
shrinking. Dirty ice bulge
has gone from the water butt;
iron has gone from the ground.
Now the weeds come, they feel the sun,
feel the slow world tilting, turning
with its burden of life, its high flying
round the round sun, undying.

Deathday

She lay cupped in white pillows
between purity of sheets
like a virgin laid in her snow;
her skin fine with a feathery softness
clinging gently to bones
at rest, her hands grained and veined
beautiful, her empty breasts
thin and small and hidden.
Brown eyes still bright she lay
watching the shifting colours of the world
tremble and dim, the humming
of voices mingled and spilled into dream;
she was waiting alone in the white sheath
of her body quietly with the quietness
of years, waiting
for strength to close her eyes against the sky
courage to rebel against the blood
for power to unclench the heart's hold,
patient to await the fires that would
submit her to the motions of the earth
that moved to bring her forth.

Contradicting the Bishop

I do not believe
my lord bishop on the BBC
in the hollowness of created things.

I am created solid, spun
right round my heart, my veins
full of crimson: no part of me
is empty, void or hollow; no not even
that female part you might call hollow
is wholly so, but is crammed
with muscle and sweet fluids,
dark fluids, tidal fluids
which I rock in me as the moon rocks
the sea that rocks the world.

Does the sea sound hollow to you?
Swim for a while in its thick salt
embrace, and dip your head
down to its swarming voices. Listen. Hear
the falling echoes of your own voice, lord,
in empty vaults, in stone-enclosed spaces
your sad belief created.

That old proud cold belief,
cutting you off from this encircling earth
ground of our being, with its core of fire.
Trees with their core of sap, hills
with their core of creatures, fruit
with its core, its seeds. Will you
not taste it? Or does your god proclaim
the hollowness of apples?

My lord, the darkest hollow
in this created world is teeming

with beings visible and invisible;
the air is full of sound, of droplets.

Flat, empty, wombless man
who sees the earth as flat
as himself, don't be afraid —
be whole, not hollow, holy, hale;
don't be forever staring
into old tombs and seeing nothingness.
Nature abhors a vacuum: there must
be life, good lord, even in Heaven,

which I do believe
(my suffering bishop) is a created thing.

Wrinkles

The wrinkle words: their silent W
that is not quite silent, but jumps at you
from the page, draws your mouth into an OO
without sound, that obsolete expletive.

All wrinkle words move, bend and twist:
I wring my hands so, with a turning wrist;
wretched I bow down, wrenching with my fist
at an old burden I can't be rid of.

I wrap a shawl around me: or my arms
around you. I wreak havoc, cause alarms;
bending and twisting, my huge wrath harms
and heals, shoots up, dies back and rankles.

I wrest this from your grasp; and we
wrangle, we wrestle, and you wriggle free:
we were both wrong, we turned perpetually
against the grain, we whirled in cross orbits.

Easy to wreck a world, to twist it out
of shape. With rapid skills we wrought
great wonders, turned our hands, but bent our
                                    thoughts
awry; we wrought ruin, crooked changes.

As I write this, the words bend to and fro
like curling sea-wrack at the rim of a slow
wave: growing clouds beyond my window
writhe through the air. My thoughts are blown
                                    wraiths.

I watch the glass. I pull a wry face:
new wrinkles ruck and ripple, mark the place
where I've been wroth, or worried. I can trace
a wreathe of smiles woven around my eyes.

Our crazy English spelling — those weird words
with odd unspoken letters and absurd
anachronisms! Here's an old-fashioned bird,

a wren. Her song, too, spirals, runs, and wrinkles.

The Cruellest Month

April, 1986

This long, cold spring, this refusal
of growth and heat: just a few bitter weeds
clenched hard on the ground, and rain
gone brutal, slubbed with sleet. We all
look desperate. Our eyes are wide and white
from watching the news, our faces shut and grey
against the weather. Snow on the high ground.
The last days — it feels like the last days:
a summer we have longed for, that never comes;
life shrunk back in on itself. Crows feeding
close to the house. Children kept in, subdued,
backs to a blear window. Waiting. Waiting.

If spring would come, if the future would only come
to relieve the present, these familiar gales
blowing from town to town; if the post should bring
those long-awaited letters; if the world
should suddenly get sick of itself, and change —
but there's no change, only wind from the north-east
gusting day after day. It's like the end
of innocence, those simple former years
when summer followed winter, when the young
grew up to adulthood in the old way,
looked forward to it. Now the fighting planes
take off, like birds of doom. Come summer, come.

Change of Season

Now the time comes round again,
time of lengthening days
April blowing towards May
sharp cries of lambs in the cold hills
yellow shocks of daffodils
and the river clears and quickens;
it's now I miss you, looking out
for you as the grass greens and thickens
and the willow points its leaves
at a high summer hanging in the wind.

Spring sun picks out my memories, spun
full of you as ever, and I learn that love
never really dies, only waits in its wings
for a change of season.

The Song of Blodeuwedd on May Morning

Skilful woman am I
and dancing woman am I
turning and turning on the green
skin of the dawn fields:
woman of light am I, my morning eyes
too clear, too bright for you.

With calmness, with care,
with breastmilk, with dew,
my web I weave
my spell I cast on you.

With calmness, a still point
that the world spins around
I am pulled up out of the ground
my spell has found you.

Beauty above and below me,
beauty behind and before me,
beauty surrounds me
and I sound, I resound like a drum.
I am making my magic, my power;
flying woman who soars to the sun
am I, lovely Goddess woman
covered in rainbows, in feathers, in flowers.
Dark my mind with visions of stars
of the night I have seen, where I have been:
See! I have chosen you.

Strong young man, a man of trees
of river-shadows, of hills, of horns;
all new and secret, my moon-mate,
I await you on the cold breeze

that brings you to me stumbling warm
from your bed, oh yes, with care,
with milk and with dew
I draw you to me on my white thread.

When you hear my voice, my cry
when you see the oak blossoming
when you feel the owls pass by
fetch your staff and run from your door —
it is I, woman of flowers, who calls
who holds wide her wings for you.
With beauty behind, with beauty before;
with calmness, with care,
with breastmilk, with dew
this stone I place: I bathe my face
and I wait for you.

Day Beginning

This morning, warm and sleepy, wearing
the sun alone we lay tousled
and tender, motionless
but for slow motions of hands
passing over and over
lazily, lighter than dust;
lying so close on the crumpled bed
where night had been hot
and clumsy, we caressed
without heat in the pure
light from the windows. Still the faint
sweat-scent, sweet and salt on sheets
and skin, but fading: wideawake
yet clasped by sleep we were quiet-breathing
and aware. Time and the golden
morning ticked away. Cool and smooth
our bodies reflected the patterns of the sun,
our minds without fear or fever reflected
each other: no past, no future,
we lay at the beginning of our day.

Photography

Sun easing west towards the treeline
ridge now full of summer
in tissues of leaf and gold
flowering on Blaenblodau hill
where every dusk of the year I see
the day fade

I in my sloping garden
which catches the slant of light and flares
green
watch my children play against the blaze
their small brown limbs shadowed
as earth this warm time

their heads crowned with fire
shaping hollow voices like birds
framed in a backdrop of hills
and I adjust the eye
of my camera because I must keep
this instant sharp

as they turn around
with arms raised and the sun
falls imperceptibly

I have taken it.

Summer Solstice

Sun, stand still:
burn
as the chestnuts burn
over the dark stream
in pure honey white flames;
swell
as the hedges swell
out over the roads
rough loaded with life —
fizzing wild carrot, cow parsley,
pink shocks of campion
and roses
buttercups polished up and bold
among sorrel, and deep grasses,
insects and beasts and birds
O sun

stand, burn, swell, excel —
before the turning
of the world
lets winter in
ashes and cold.

As you wait in prime time
we watch
we touch eye to eye.
The pouring down of your gold
is endless, endless:
the world's green
is full of it, brimming with fire;
the world's water
hums with it, a live wire,
a wild womb
holding you, moulding your power.

So we watch
we touch, we hold
on, hold on
scarce daring to stir;
like the oak's
slow ripple of new wood,
its breathing leaves.

Sun
keep still
beautiful
this drop, this flower, this flesh,
the dusk's long blaze
these meadows rolled in dew
dawn mist touching my window;
and summer, summer
keep always still
like a spark
a warm scent in the dark
as the grey days
unfold.

The Trespasser

My fingers are sweet with stealing
blackcurrants. Among tall weeds
ropes of them, thick and ripe like secrets.
I move in shadow, sharp-eyed, listening.
A distant car sets my spine quivering.
Bold as a bird I pull the berries down,
gather them in. Their smell excites me.

The house is blind: no-one is living here,
yet I am trespassing. Each summer the owners
come for a week or two, cut grass,
clean windows, stare out from their gate.
But the river sings all year; and swifts make
nests, flowers bloom and fruit
ripens, and snow sweeps the lawn
smooth for the prints of foxes.

In spring there were daffodils, massed gold
and white narcissi; I ran in the rain
to gather armfuls, carrying them home
to shine in my windows. I live by here
every day, in poverty. What the hedges grow,
what's in the hills, I take back for my children.

Great polished blackcurrants in my fist.
They drop in the bag, grow fat.
Tonight I'll mix them with sugar, and steam
them slowly. The dark, sour, smoky taste;
my children's red mouths and chins,
their high, bird voices. Each year the trees
step forward round the house: I notice that.
In the autumn, I'll come for apples.

The Child's House

The house is the centre.
Tall and wide
it pulls upwards from the earth,
curving slightly, its roots hidden.

The windows shine outwards:
there is no looking in
those intense, vibrant squares
nor through the vagueness of the door.

So steeply the roof
is tiled, solidly
giving shelter, and the chimney
smokes, a life message.

Where have I seen
flowers like these dream flowers,
or such a sun
pouring down like water?

What are these shapes
of birds in the brickwork,
in the body of the house
or flying over it, blessing?

Or the tree with twigs outspread
like fingers, to catch
at the brilliant rays
and the blest shapes of the birds?

A circular shining
and bending
and curled colours
gladden this brushed vision,

this wholeness, this world
daubed in an hour;
this loved, lost country
left drying on the bench.

Salt Creek

Warm late afternoon of long sun
where the tall masts dipped in distance
in this strange salt place of winds
and the unseen sea, this place of grass,
summer shook its seeds.

A lark hung like a flung stone
in the sky that is always changing
wings vibrant, voice shrill and high
in the acres of the wide sky,

and behind, the thud of dredgers
ceaseless and softened beyond the banks.
Grass, splashed thick with clover, smelled sweet
as the afternoon fell slowly into the ground.

Insects flickered above and between the blades.
I stood on a high place over a creek
where a man was wading, back bent, hand in water,
the flat land blowing behind;

and the wind was so clean and the sun so rich
I stretched my arms outwards and cried,
I could live forever.

The bowed man in the creek never straightened or
                                    stirred
his head, but bent waterwards down
and the dead weeds in the creek were brown and still.

When my Baby Looks at Trees

When my baby looks at trees he sees
the wind's shape;
his face becomes still
as the branches sway and dip
for his delight, as the bright
sky dances through. He stares,
his nose twitches at leaf
and resin, sour bark, sweet earth,
the juices in the wood.

If he could climb trees
he'd be out of my arms and up
in the creaking heights
laughing among the leaves;
and his white hands move jerkily
trying to touch. What he sees
is the glow of the sap as it spreads
out and upwards, the shine
of the tree's breath.

His eyes widen and darken
and lighten to green;
a smile brushes his mouth
and cheek, and a look
passes light between him and the tree.
He is close in my arms, but apart.
When we turn to go
his skin smells of forests, he holds
his face to the wind.

Bodhrán

I shall take the drum
with both my hands
and beat a madness around

a roaring, a sound
of thunder
rolled in my palms

rocking between my arms
a live heart
rich with the thump of blood.

I shall bend the wood
of a sapling, the skin of a goat
pulled hard and tight

and take it out every night
for the moon
to shape it and shrink it.

Think of it
as my madness
the drumming of rage

or my coming of age
savage joy
beating flesh with a bone

for I've always known
it would happen
I've known it would come

the time of the drum.

It's pounding seas
it's a swarm of bees
it's a storm of rain
it's a dish of grain
it's a womb of blood
it's a tomb of mud
it's a leather shield
it's a sown field

a bear's strength
an owl's stealth
an arm's length
from my deep self

it's the shaman in me
shaman in me
step to my tune
and you'll see.

If You Should Come To My House

If you should come to my house
warm with walking in the cold dusk
of the afternoon, walking quickly
being far too impatient to catch the bus,
to arrive at last all windswept at my door
with your white breath about you, if
you should knock suddenly
while I was making coffee just for
one, or cleaning out my cluttered room
in readiness for a chance visitor like you,
I'd run to meet you down every stair;
I'd fling my door wide to you, and soon
you would be sitting here
with my coffee in your hands, the whole place
in a muddle, but music on, and you'd feel
the fire's warmth on your face;
just supposing that you should come
out of the blowing leaves and autumn smoke
bright copper in the dropping sun, out
of the wind to my house and to my room
I would never turn you out into the rain:
I would greet you with a smile and take your coat
happy to sit you in my one chair,
and never shut my eyes to you again.

Winter Solstice

It is quiet here
And warm, never mind
The wind beyond this room
Unfastening the last leaves;
Dark afternoons
Seagulls floating above the lawns,
Mornings of cold sunlight in puddles
Bright-cheeked in fur;
It is peaceful here
Like lying after love in one huddle
Sleepily, while windows tremble
And night pours down the glass.

But the hour approaches:
The year is withering
Into the blackness behind the last
Star; then we shall all
Make war against the cold.
I must walk out alone
Into the bitter snow
With Gawain in his journey,
When from the sanctuary
Of the jewelled court he rode
After the shrivelled sun.

No easy motorway
Northwards into the storm:
He went through a dead world,
Searching for knowledge
In dank tangled woods.
That winter journey!
Snow-black hung the sky,
Snow stretched wet on the hills,
Stung in the flaking wind.

Pursuing his smudged track
I must struggle out now
As the sap shrinks back to the root;
An untried sword about me,
My mind crowded with stories
I ride to meet myself.

An Invocation to Pan

Come, eye of the forest
come, beast-footed
stag-crowned
man-membered; come, tree-sinewed
soil-rubbed, leaf-garlanded;
come, goat-nimble
come, bird-joyful
come, fox-cunning;
out of the boles and burrows
out of the humps and hollows
out of the heaps of leaves;
out of mist and darkness
out of sunshafts, gold motes,
flowers, insects humming:
brown lying down in summer by the river
your flute notes cool
and black striding up from the woods in winter
wreathed in fogs, your voice belling;
come, old one, come, green one,
tree-protector, beast-befriender
good shepherd, wise steward:
come, earth-brother
long long lost
long long lost
let us find you
call you
call you up, out, back, forth —
be here now!
O musk of fur sour
in the wind, your branched head
through the thickets
coming, coming
in your power, your power, your power.

Hunting the Wren

The boys are out in the frost.
Redeyed pack in the black sticks
of the wood, crunching tracks,
shaking snow
from shoved-aside branches;
faces rubbed raw
poor boys
numb and raw with cold
purplish fingers grabbing.
They are coming this way
fists bright with holly
who run and tiptoe and follow
under a bloody sun:
Milder and Molder
and Jackie the Can
and Johnny Red Nose
and everyone.

They are coming this way
treading dead leaves
empty trees overhead.
They roll in laughter
but under the their black jackets
they brandish
death;
their smiles hide
the lanterns, the hollow box,
the toothed snares.
They are after blood in the wood.
Shabby bandits
in the gathering dusk
drunk with good hunting
they come, they come.

Their burden is heavy
as they climb the slow hill
towards town,
the box all ribboned around
which they hold
turn and turn
about, as owls come out.
Rough boys with stony faces
now graced with heroes' eyes
in the twilight, in pride
of the deed done.

Hours spent scouring the hills
and the forest thorns
since morning crept over
slate roofs and ponds:
all for the sake of an old song
and dance, stories
of questing for dragons
the black boar
of old winter, tusked with ice.
Only the best
beast of the wood
will do to die
till spring shines.
Away from good food and warm fires
they spent the day with monsters
fought over bushes and briars —
they struggled, they won.

The last rays of the brief day
follow the noisy crew
with their garland box
that rattles like a nut

with the fruit of all their daring:
a handful of feathers
a spoonful of blood.
Good luck
drink up
a new year has begun!

says Milder to Molder
says Jackie the Can
says Johnny Red Nose
says everyone.

Book of Shadows

TWO RIVERS

To the Islands

Driving to Llanybydder from the hills
in sunlight, a clean blue sky
bathing us in its image: a light-pocket,
an open eye in all those weeks of rain,

we suddenly saw the sea in a strange place,
inland. We followed a new coast:
pale lucid water filled the low ground
to the west, and risen islands stood

netted with fields or thinly brushed
with trees; and shoreside cottages
whitewashed, perched over a harbour —
a landscape from the inner Hebrides

exact and stunning. Though of course we knew
it was only a trick of mist, sucked up
from unremarkable sodden earth, still
we cried out happily: "Look at the sea!"

So it shall be someday, when the polar ice
melts, and expanding oceans lift
over the land again. Sea licking
these hills into islands and promontories

the Teifi swallowed into a sea-loch
and lush farms drowned, the hill-farms turned
into fisherman's cottages. We could see
the future in a bowl of clear water,

seeing the present too, scrying the land
that is always there but mostly invisible —
the land's other face, the place where boats
put out from curved inlets, and green fields

tilt down to the sea; where eels thread
their way between tall hedges. Sun low
behind us, as far south as it will go
as we ran into the outer blurs of mist

and the islands vanished. Above, we sensed
the summer colour of sky without seeing it:
and, turning west, we crossed the plain grey river
in silence, like driving through water.

Feeding the Bat

At first it was a small cold palmful
a hunched and sorry scrap, clenched still
but for an infinitesimal buzz and tremble

as we passed it from hand to hand
half fearful that the buzzing might explode
into uncontrollable flight. So we found

a box, and a place by the stove, and scrounged
a spoonful of dogfood from the corner shop
and waited. When the scratching started

we crowded round to listen: it was alive!
Lifting it out, it seemed larger; it moved
its clever head from side to side, gave

delicate soundings. Two eyes, dark points of light
gleamed, not at all blind, and long questioning
fingers gripped mine. Whiskered like a cat

with a cat's silken cunning it consented
to be fed from the end of a stick, opened
a triangle mouth wide, and dipped and lunged

manoeuvring meatlumps in. Laughing, we squeezed
waterdrops onto its nose, to hear it sneeze
minute bat-sneezes, to watch the supple greedy

slip of a tongue flick the droplets down.
As it warmed, it got bolder, nipping our skin
with needle teeth, unfolding its tucked wings

turning its goblin face to the window, where
milky chilled spring daylight lured
it to sudden flight, skimming at head height

a strange slow flutter, followed by a whisper
of displaced air. Awaiting a change of weather
we hung it in a bag to sleep over the stairs

and roused it for feeding. After the second day
it arched its back to be stroked, and played
a biting game, neck stretched impossibly

backwards, slyly grinning. That evening, the sun
shone. We carried it in its bag to a vacant barn
by the river. It squealed as I left it there, long

angry squeals; but I was firm. I would not
be quite a witch yet, stroking and feeding a bat
my ears tuned to its music, swooping, flitting about —

though I lean out to the buoyant dusk, for all that.

Your Castle Picture

The sky comes right down to the ground
in your picture. And my eye's led
over scrawled grass to the castle,
solid and grey with its black slits,
its great dark ruined archways. You
have remembered a strange sight
of windows through the arch; they shine
deep blue in the crayoned shadows.

Tremendous — but is it right
that the sky should come down
all the way to the ground?
Last week, your sky was childish, high
and innocent, blue strip
at the top of the page, and white
air everywhere. I liked the way
the sun hung under it, with yellow
leggy rays. I liked the earth
swept safe beneath our feet. So
what's happened to bring the sky so low,
the earth so hunched and high?
The sun shrunk to a blurred smear
too bright to focus on?

I look at you, but your smile is clear colour,
glowing, unspoiled. There's a storm outside
blundering with charcoal clouds
I could almost paint. The sky
is close to us: it's scribbled on the ground.

Little son, as you ran shouting in the gale
I stuck your castle picture to my wall.

Life Class

Here is my arm. My weight rests
lightly, poised and yielding
to take the load of my body
while letting the blood flow;
so when the tingle begins I can
shift a little, imperceptibly
without spoiling your view of the lines
the angles and shadows.
I watch the texture of light
on the slopes of my arm, and regard
its landscape, as if for the first time.

Here are my legs. Doubled-up
my knees may present problems
of perspective. My thighs plunge
highlighted against the floor.
My trapped calves throb a little.
Soon the pain will start
to needle and stab, and I'll
breathe in rhythm, alongside,
keeping my distance.

Here is my stomach. There's a twist
in this posture, a challenge:
I am all changing planes.
The one part of me
that's visibly moving, rising
and falling as I breathe:
my belly, my centre
that cannot be still.

And my breasts, here, are just
two curves of light
and between my legs, a shadow.

Here is my head. I've tied
my hair so the stem of my neck
shows, the precise tilt,
the line between spine and brain.
I've turned my face aside
in abstraction. I prefer no
eye-contact: it jolts me back
into your world, the world
of touch and movement.
So I arrange my gaze
on a picture, a fragment of curtain,
two wood-knots, the flesh of my arm.

A long, slow time. The scratch
and shirr of pencils on paper,
charcoal's thick squeak and whisper
clatter of brushes in water
subdued words, coughs and sighs
entertain me. I feed my mind
on all that concentration.

And yet it empties itself
constantly, it can't hold
to any thought, it must move —
or I can't keep still. It turns
and shifts, it is shrouded,
veiled: you can't draw it,
it's not available. My body
is public as the body of a tree
but my mind's private, goes
walkabout, darts like a bird.

Though there's one thought
returning, over and over.
How I am shameless
before strangers, before
their intimate gaze, yet
when my lover said, Stand up —
walk round the room; I want
to look at you — yes turn
like that... why did I blush
move stiffly, rapidly,
and cover myself with laughter?

Moving the Boxes

(for Anabel)

This was the least I could give you:
My strength on the far side of a box
Packed with your hidden life, the weight
Of cheerful clutter, our years apart.
Our backs and arms were strong
Together, making a dance of it.

I pushed the sides shut, and you taped
All joins and edges tight against time
And weather; our eyes met over the stacks,
We laughed a lot. You folded summer clothes
For a distant season. It was work, tough
Labour, pressing the grief right down.

It was the last I could give you:
A catkin branch from the river, a clutch
Of snowdrops, their white winged faces;
My scrubbing-out of cupboards, scratch
Meals from the ends of packets, a spread
Of coloured cards, chances, changes.

And for me, the gathering-up of love
Giving me heart again. We could see
Each other now quite clearly without our men:
Our perfect, matched movements, our double
                              power.
It was no trouble. The boxes are well-filled;
Now for the hard part. We'll share the load.

Through the Walls

Old Jock is crying through the walls again.
Yesterday I saw him in his garden
bayoneting weeds
staking sweet peas to attention:
and then a slow fourth coat of paint to the fence.

He is lying on the carpet in his swept
parlour, a teacup smashed
at his side, and Missus sped
downhill to the telephone.
He murders his pain. His walls are red
tartan, Crawford colours, biscuit tins.

Last night, we heard them come in
from the club: the slam
of doors, his parade-ground yell.
We sniggered under bedclothes, listening.
Inches from our heads
his teenage son sobbed, sobbed
as Jock ran out in the street, hurling dark
obscenities after the grown one.
Missus begged peace,
made tea and sandwiches as the moon set.

"They wrote me off" he said, and his false teeth
clamped on a smile; "but I'm a bonny fighter."
His eyes were wild blue, the pupils ringed
with death. "I canna eat
since they cut the guts from me" — but he wolfed
his biscuits, chewed soft white bread.
Missus takes care of him. The heavy smell
of mutton cloys our cupboards.

"Did you hear him scream?" she asked me
last time, rosy with pride. And now
there's a crash of falling chairs, and the ragged shouts
of battle. Soon an ambulance will stop
outside, to a flicker of curtains.

An enemy cat prowls in the drill lines
of his borders. I watch the wall.

A Concert of Chinese Music
on Radio Three

rare, delicious sun
mingles with the water notes
of a Chinese flute

frost on the windows
disassembling its fronds
gently, easily

to a sound of gongs
the Dragon of Spring set loose
on Khingan mountain

in these cold Welsh hills
I call a five-pointed scale
and watch the sun come

House

I will live in a House
By the Side of the Road
& Be a Friend to Man
(John Crowley: *Little, Big*)

House of irregular stones
House of sparkling quartz fragments
House roofed with split slate

Low house backed onto a wet field
With a generous yellow door
A cobbled yard studded with dandelions
And in winter, stacked with cut logs

House in the flightpath of gales
House blown about with mist
House with the wind in its walls

A cramped untidy house, dark
As a shed with a view
Of great western cloudscapes
The voice of December in its broad chimney

House forged in primal fire
House of resinous flame
House whose stones store summer

Whose narrow windows catch the slow
Movement of sun along the ridge
The slide across seasons, the shift
Of light on our faces each morning

House polished by rain
House of brimming gutters
House with its roots in water

Its floorstones shaped in a river
Scud of ripples on their washed faces
House shod with fossil mud and waveprints
Wading through water like a stone ship

House of uneven timbers
House of broad ancient planks
House that creaks in the wind

Its ceiling beams filched from a wrecked vessel
Its oak lintels bowed with the weight of years
Sawdust trodden into the hall carpet
And woodsmoke heavy in the furnishings:

Though its windows are deep and small
They show us an immensity of stars
And the stars seem small from our immensity
And time a poem made in the walls of a house

Under Eaves Wood

night still crouched, and the track
fell steeply into shadow.
We followed, our minds full of sleep

but our feet exact and sure
over mud and black stone outcrops.
Below, the brimming trough

of the valley, starred with lights;
and ahead, a slim moon
burned and tilted in infinity.

Two figures hurrying through dawn
under the weight of the hills, the trees'
crowded terrace, not looking

but feeling their way through
the wood's still life. The air
was charged; it sparked with hope

the cool blue tingle of a good day.
My bag bumped at my shoulder. You moved
before me, swift as a cat

through the open door of morning.
For each of us, without judgement,
Eve's blessing on our path, our way.

Two Rivers

It was here, in the long red meadow
two princes fought a battle
in old times, in the shadow
beneath this hill
in this dark sorrel
where children roll and squeal
flattening pathways in the brushed grass.
This ridge, the high seat
its flank woods heavy with summer —
was this where he raised his spear,
stood lightly rehearsing the blow

while the villagers swarmed below
with pop and crisps and bright-striped folding
chairs, men in tweed caps, woman
in pale blue nylon housecoats
faces pink in an unaccustomed sun?

And the one they fought for — was she
there in the crowd with her schoolfriends
pressed round her, craning for a sight
of blood? Or sitting high
as a bird, like a Carnival Queen?
Or did she stand alone with her hair down,
her fingers twisting together, down by the river
to her knees in plumes of meadowsweet?

I think she turned her face when the blow fell
and the crowd yelled and horns blared
towards the place where the two rivers meet.

Two rivers, brown and muscled, struggle
endlessly in a pool. Warm afternoons
in our own short summer, I've gone there
to skinny-dip, the shock
of water raising up gooseflesh.
Feeling the two floods not quite equally cold:
      one with a little sun in it
      one with the mountain in it
and my body between the two
touching them both, as she once used to do.

Was it here, to this shadowed pool
when the show was over
she fled with her nine maidens
pursued by red-faced men, her triumphant lover?
Along the footpath from the post office
they ran to fetch her; but she'd flown
with her white turned face into the alder scrub
in a flurry of wings and claws.

Now they have lost her in the long
meadow; and their darkness is complete.

She flies high
here, in the woods, at night —
I've heard her thin cry, where the rivers meet.

A World Elsewhere

My daughter stood in the sunlight, winnowing grain.
I sat at her feet, looked upwards: she was strong
astride in her blue dress, her forearms busy.
The chaff scattered, sailing down to me
on the threshing-floor. A hilltop breeze
ruffled in through the doors, from the world
of summer. Her youngest daughter curled
asleep on my lap, dark in my nestled crook.

Chaff coming down like light; the rattling grain
in its round skin tray; and a sound
of singing from the hill. Such a strong blue
sky out there: in here, a gold sifting.
The barley-smell. Smell of my daughter's sweat.
Warm weight of the child against my bones.

I sat in moving shadows, and I laughed:
throaty, low — an old woman's privilege.
Throaty, low, in the dusty winnowing,
the floating husk, sun motes. To think
of all we'd journeyed through! Of how
I'd carried them with me, children and seeds
of children, through years of horror, to arrive
here. Through poison, cold and hunger, through
the infected City, blood and guns, despair
to arrive here. Above, the wide circle
of shaking grain. Outside, cut straws
in an August sun. Birch saplings starting up
from the ruins of a town. My grandchildren.
She turned to look at me. "There's loads to do
Mum, and you sit there cackling."
The small girl shifted, opened a brown eye slowly.
My daughter, cooling in her blue dress, smiled.

Brynberllan

This is a place where nothing really grows
but water: water and stones.

And concrete bungalows, and lost holdings.

Tilt of water from the mountainside
pushes under the road, and stones grow
overnight in our gardens: rainbuffed hard
perennials. We're on the flank
of the wind, even in summer.

But years ago, this was an apple orchard.

Rows and patterns of trees, all the way
down to the stream called *Comely*;
mossy barked, their darkblue stems at dusk,
the sun spread white at dawn on slopes
of blossom; warm air, stirred thick
with honey. Humming and swarms, and then
the smell of ripe fruit: those small
sharp western apples.

Crowded faces, bushes and basketfuls.

Everyone there, at work in the branches,
measuring the loads, brownarmed
and busy. Shouts in the crisp leaves.
Children rolling windfalls down the hill.
Foxes nosing at night through bruised grass.

And apple smoking in the soul-fires.

I think the traffic worsens year by year
just passing through. Rain's harsher too:

laced with acid and caesium, it fills
the stream called *Comely* and the stream
called *Blossom*. Nothing flourishes.

Yet sometimes we'll distill, between breath

and breath, a taste of sweetness:
yes, even now, a rustling of leaves
a blossom-drift. Between low flakes
of October sunlight, treeshapes flicker;
and evenings to the West bring cloud-landscapes
rising like a range of wooded hills,
a place of apple-orchards. Not here: beyond

reach, elsewhere, forsaken, forfeited.

Llanthony Priory

It's a heathen rain today
driving over the high pass from Hay
falling in blown webs and torn shreds
over great weights and sacred elevations
raised to withstand the weathers of the world
now letting the wet world in;

falling on arches propping up the wind
falling on these stumps of sure foundation
falling in smoke-drift down the long nave
falling like a shaken benediction

over the damp chancel and shattered tower
over the drip, drip in the canons' kitchen
over the lost cloister and buried choir:

an irreligious rain. We stand in its lee
by a bit of stacked buttress.

Geese in a little paddock stuck with trees
stretch their rude necks at us. My children
yelling and running down the green slope
of the altar steps, chase round the sanctuary.
And in the prior's lodging, yellow elder
waggles her sexy fruits.

The ruins shape our gaze; they lift
our eyes to the hills: from whence cometh rain.
The immanent and omnipresent hills
which were always there, during lauds and vespers
a mighty unseen eminence, like God
waiting beyond the walls. And now
they've broken though that careful masonry
in a pantheon, tremendously circled,
splendidly photogenic, framed in stone.

I lift my camera, and wander round
to capture an alignment. Dewi's rain
gusts down from Wales, floating in fine drops
in your pagan hair. Our Lady pours
dark red in rivers from the mountainside
chanting perpetual sorrows. Holy wells
are rising. Litanies and psalms
from vivid, potent, scarlet tongues of bracken.

These sharpedged, lovely lines
are spare and windswept, leave us comfortless.
You huddle in your coat. Let's go back soon,
and sample the real ale at the Half Moon.

The Little Cloth

The odour of sanctity. Candles
their clear warm waxy spirits,
fresh cut blooms in paschal yellows and white,
bitter incense swung by a solemn boy,
the smell of washed Sunday bodies.

I was fifteen: I had waited a long time.

I knelt between mother and sister.
The priest moved his hands like a doll
decked out in ivory and gold for Easter.
Latin today: charmed occult syllables
long rustling silences, the soft chink of censers,
altar boys, white lace, male mysteries.

Sleepily I watched my own candle dip
and shrink in its fiery terrace
under the virgin's peeling plaster toes.
I hugged an unusual dragging ache, a tightness.

Sometimes I thought I might become a saint
to go into ecstasy and talk with angels;
not worry about my figure, my crop of spots
but to live in a forest hut on wild herbs
breathing wisdom like clean air.

The bell's small icy note
startled me back: the white moon
of the host raised up, then the chalice.
This is my blood, he said, and drank,
and wiped the cup. When that cloth is washed
(a priest once told me) the woman
must be in a state of grace
and the water not tipped down the sink
but emptied on the ground — just think of it.

My grandmother washed and washed little bloody
cloths.

Ecce Panis Angelorum a woman sang
from the choir, her voice sexless and pure.
Strong vowels responded: I felt a loosing
of knots, a moist unfolding
from darkness, my chalice filled with blood

and the gold eyes of every angel turned
towards me, and I burned
with sudden grace, and my moon-Jesus rose
from the shadows and saw me. I was a saint at last —
my blood poured out for you
and for many; my new huge pride.

The soft white secret cloth
between my legs, reminded me all day.

A Northwest Passage

(A recent autopsy on the bodies of three of the members of
Lord Franklin's last expedition revealed that they died of
lead poisoning from contaminated tinned food.)

Franklin's seaman lies in a dream of ice:
his brain's turned into an oval lump
of solid ice. It fills
his skull with a cloudy whiteness.

His body is unchanging, six feet
down in the permafrost. He has forgotten
sunlight through green leaves,
tartness of orchard apples, the warm
loam of Kent. In his cells
an Arctic silence. His last thoughts frozen.

What made them sew him up
warmly in all his shirts? Was it
to keep him from the cold?
Why did they struggle with clumsy picks
ringing on frozen gravel, hour after hour
in shrieking winter darkness
chipping and spitting ice, to make graves?

Was it love, in that awful place?

This decent, graceful gift:
a red cloth laid like a prayer
over his face, hiding the terrible clamp
of pain, the lips drawn back
over uneven teeth, the eyes locked.
Too tall for the hasty coffin, they crammed him in
with one arm twisted beneath him.

John Torrington, John Hartnell, William Braine:
abandoned with their chiselled names
in a dead time, poison in their bones
and guts, and hair. In Arctic time

the wind is a true presence:
the sky is the world
surrounding a small circle of shifting ice.

And the names of the trapped ships
Terror and *Erebus*
are a dreadful presence; and the names
of Franklin and his crew
dragging the weight of a slow death
blindly over the snow, daft wanderers
searching for a way through

stumbling into the sun, are a presence.

The Sealwife

One day I shall find my skin again:
my own salt skin, folded dark, its fishweed stink
and tang, its thick warm fat, great thrusting tail

all mine: and I'll take it and shake it out
to the wind, draw it over me cool and snug,
laugh softly, and slip back to my element.

I shall find my stolen skin, hidden by you
for love (you said) that night the sea-people danced,
stashed in some cleft in the rocks where I may not go

but used to go, and dance too, stepping free
in my new peeled body, the stalks of my legs in the moon-
light strange, my long arms shaping the sky

that have narrowed their circles down
to the tasks of these forked hands: lifting,
fetching, stirring, scrubbing, embracing — the small

stiff landlocked movements. In the sea
I plunged and swam for my own joy, sleek and oiled,
and I loved at will in rolling-belly tides.

Here love is trapped between the walls of a house
and in your voice and eyes, our children's cries;
whose boundaries I've understood, a language

learnt slowly, word by word. You've been dear and good —
how you would sing to me, those wild nights!
— and oil my breasts by firelight, and dip down

to taste my sea-fluids. I'd forget to mourn
those others then, trawling the flickering deeps.
Now I cry for no reason, and dream of seals:

an ocean booms in the far cave of my ear
and voices tug at me as I stand here
at the window, listening. Our children sleep

and by daylight they run from me. Their legs
strong, their backs straight, bodies at ease
on solid ground — though they play for hours
                                    on the shore

between sand and sea, and scramble the wet rocks
gladly. It won't be long now, the waiting:
they love to poke and forage in the cracks

of the cliffs; sharpeyed, calling, waving.

The Bee-flight

That was a strange, rare place, in a loop
between river and nippled hill
with a crooked sandstone church and trees
that corkscrewed, and a massive leaning yew
one thousand years thick, peeled rosy flesh
and a woman carved into the north wall
with legs agape, and a man with a bird's head
whistling sorcery. The ground rose
in hummocks: the past, carelessly buried,
trying to break through. Snowdrops showed white
and wet below the mound. I stood at the cusp
of spring in a flayed landscape
bleached-out by frost, stripped clean

as an old bone, sucked dry. I'd thought
there was nothing to fill me, nothing to speak to me;
but here was rain smelling of turned earth,
the sun in watercolour, curved paths,
storybook trees, bark swirled, bulged-out and fissured
peopling the place. At the edge of a pool
a straddled oak with a hole
at eye level, forced me to stare. Birds calling, then
a humming past my ear, and again; brown bees
sailing in from the sedges, dipping down
into darkness, hollow mouth-oak, in and in
with grains of new gold. A ragged shower blew
up from the west. Something unfolding, stirring

under my feet. The lumpy, breast-topped crag
now spiralled in light; the birdman suddenly answered
by choruses of wings, and the opened thighs
of the sandstone witch by the presence of flying bees.

Breakfast with the Poets

Dawn at the Alcazaba.
The poets come
up from the drowsy city, appearing like birds
from a woven nest of alleys
some walking, most in cars
turning difficult corners in the dark
all drawn to the honey rock

in scores, in hundreds
from under stones, on a breeze from the desert,
the folds of the sea. They've come
with spouses, friends and children, greeting
each other on the steps of the citadel
of light. That woman in evening dress
hasn't slept all night. That child,
like ours, stares through us,
eyes blank with dreams. They climb
and we climb with them
through the sultan's exquisite garden
shaping word after word.

Up in the high courtyard
are men with microphones, women
trailing long veils. Everyone laughs, delighted.
We lean together over rose-coloured walls
and watch the sun
rise over stripped hills, ruined terraces.
This is a strange country
breeding poets instead of flies. They swarm
in the pure, steady light.

They hand out dazzling blankets:
like loaves and fishes, it's a miracle —
everyone sits down. Music swells
in a wild, muezzin cry.

A woman lifts brown arms, releasing
a pigeon. *See, I have laid*
my greeting in the collar of a dove
which will fly over the land
of Almería like a flung censer.

The poets read in turn
women and men, intensely
darkly and gloriously. Children wriggle:
I can't understand
all the words either; but they seem
poems of celebration.

Morning expands and blazes; the sun hits
the wall above us with a gold fist.
The city is awake: it roars
and glitters in the wilderness; a bucket
of whitewash thrown at the mountains.
Comrade poets, ladies, gentlemen,
now breakfast will be served:
herb tea and spicecakes in the high tower
of Ibn Al-Mu'tasim.

Andarax

(Almería, Andalusia)

On the map, a broad blue sinuous line said
water. Dark, fluid and cool
from the snows of the Sierra Nevada,
bordered by orange groves and thirsty vines
threading and falling, a ripple between banks

because in Wales a river means moving water
I pictured that. So nothing prepared me for
nothing — that yawning ditch of dust,
that void, that absence. Sun spat
and crackled in the stones. Baked mud

cracked open. A long bridge spanned
the gulf. Everything the bleached-out dun
of old shit. On a ruinous site nearby
a JCB dug slowly: the dust went ten feet down —
further, the whole way. Crossing the no-river,

crossing the Andarax, I shuddered; my throat
dry as a lizard's, my eyes peeled raw.
Down to bedrock. Even its name's a cough,
a rasp, a drought. It does not summon liquid,
shadowy pools, slack shallows, slide of fish.

It's the name of a slaughtered dragon;
a mythical beast; a fossil; a chained Book
of Spells, with dark parchment pages: *Andarax*.
Somebody mentioned a winter legend of water,
snow-floods. I could not believe it:

that was too long ago, in another country.

BOOK OF SHADOWS

"Because ideas are the basic forms of things, according to which everything is made... we should create in ourselves the shadows of ideas... in order to shape them to all possible realities. We create them in us, images revolving like wheels. If you know any other way, try it."
(Giordano Bruno: *On the Shadows of Ideas* [Paris, 1582])

"Doctor Jordano Bruno Nolano, a professor in philosophy, intends to pass into England; whose religion I cannot commend."
(Henry Cobham, English Ambassador in Paris, 1583)

To Begin With....

The shadows of ideas are the stuff of poetry. They are the symbols and metaphors we use to express reality: they are language itself, in which each word is a symbol, the shadow of an idea, a *spell* by which we gain some power in the world, able to shape our will and direct it.

Four hundred years ago the connection between poetry and magic was more directly understood than it is today. The power of words to change lives was respected and feared. Our ancestors also understood the importance of imagery, the ability to directly visualise a memory or an idea, in order to make it real. So dreams could be turned to reality, ideas could begin to affect the external world. And the mysterious and awesome powers that controlled the Universe and the workings of Nature could, they believed, be drawn into oneself and used.

Such were the dreams and ideas behind a fantastic out-pouring of creativity in the European Renaissance. That belief in the power of human imagination to change the world, the excitement of rediscovering a mythical golden age of wisdom and looking forward to a visionary future, a new age, was the driving force behind the great paintings and music, architecture and literature of those times.

When the new ideas challenged the status quo too directly, their expounders were likely to get burned. Such a free-thinker who met with a grisly end was the 16th century philosopher, magician and poet Giordano Bruno. It was only to be expected: not only did he claim that the earth and the whole of Nature was alive and divine, not only did he propose that the earth moved around the sun in a boundless universe of suns and worlds, but he predicted the fall of the Christian order and its replacement with a new religion based on a revival of paganism: the 'Religion of the World'.

You can read more about Bruno and his ideas in the Notes at the end of this book. His vision and his character are the impetus behind this sequence of poems; the poems are my response from our own times of change. They are not really about Giordano Bruno and the 16th century — many better and factual books have been written about that. Although Bruno appears here, I must stress again: these poems are not about him.

They are about us.

They are about the world we live in now, and the issues we face now; which, strangely enough, are the same old issues, but differently dressed.

Occasionally Bruno may appear to take centre stage, speaking in his own voice, and several poems turn on incidents in his life. Other poems are more directly in my own voice; while others are deliberately ambiguous. I am not writing about history, but about what concerns us all: the world we live in, our environment — physical, spiritual, emotional.

Moving through the coded rich symbolism of the Tarot Trumps, I link Bruno's archaic worldview with our own, and discover strange parallels. I explore the old relationship between poetry and magic, and between magic and love, and understand that it has never been broken.

HLW Pencader 1989

O
Nola

In my childhood, I thought nothing existed beyond Vesuvius
(*De Immenso*)

Now I understand, I understand everything.
Birds' eggs are small pieces of sky;
the chicks inside are stolen from the wind

and the wind blows because the trees move it
with their dancing leaves: they move the lake too
into waves. And I know where night is made:

in the lake, from black stones in the mud there.
Dark breathes out and rises from the water,
and daylight every morning moves the leaves.

In those trees by the river, mothers find their babies;
I've seen them walking into the woods with baskets
on windy afternoons. Today I helped Mamma

pick bilberries. She said I'm sharp as a bird.
I know about angels, too: they live in the Sun,
but they visit Nola sometimes secretly

streaming down in bars of light — they look like specks
but they're really huge, huge. Here's my cave
where I talk to them, and leave them figs and flowers:

in the morning there's nothing left, so I know they
                                        love me.
Can you see that dark hump where the world ends?
We call it Vesuvius, the shadow mountain;

nobody lives there, it's too black and cold —
not like our green mountain, with goats and sheep
and Uncle Taddeo's hut, and the white track

up to the summer pasture. There's our holy well
with its chained cup, and light in the water
rolling around like a snake to make you strong.

And I have discovered bee-swarms in the earth:
I've heard them when I lie in the June grass
on hot still days, humming under my head,

under my hands, down in the earth's hive —
or is the world buzzing? That deep, thick honey voice,
her soil, her stones, alive. See! I understand.

I
Book of Shadows

Behold now, before you, the man who has pierced the air
and penetrated the sky, journeyed among the stars and
soared beyond the margins of the world...

(La Cena dei Ceneri)

Under the shadow of the good and true
I am feeling, groping my way through an inner room
a mole in a mass of roots, no a fish among weeds
seeing and touching in silence by greenshift sun.
Holding it all, holding it all together:
gathering up, mending the smashed mirror
seven-thousand-years' bad luck; and here's the one
clear perfect image, the crazed world newly reflected
turning in unison, its scattered notes
tumbling into a song — now then, hold on
to that mirror image — building, joining-up
atom to atom in the universe
in a great golden chain. The bee flies out

from its close monastic cell, never having seen
flowers, but having an image of flowers
somewhere imprinted, sees and smells and knows
the source of sweetness, burrowing with joy
and bringing treasure home. I am a bee.
The different colours of flowers do not confuse me.

So I make, comb by comb, my magic book —
a Book of Shadows. Its pages flicker and gleam
as if seen underwater; its letters red and black,
its curious diagrams, mad conjurations
scud in and out of light, unreadable.
But as I draw it slowly from the pool
of Imagination, look! It becomes plain, easy.
This is magic; what I do. I have come to you

with the world up my sleeve and heaven in my hat
shuffling a clutch of pictures. On my pied robe
I've sewn the stars invisible: they are inside,
within, where they should be — Luna and Sol,
Mercury, Bootes, the Bull, the Banquet.

Now shut your eyes. I can make you see them too:
stars in a meadow, knuckles on a tree,
galaxy shells, lost cities at low tide
shouldering out of the slime. Hold it all, all
precious and rare, mind-mirror, dazzling round
Book of infinite pages, colours, shadows and sound.

II
Athene

Her have I loved and sought from my youth, and desired
for my spouse, and have become a lover of her form...
and I prayed... that she might be sent to abide with me,
that I might know what I lacked... for she knew and
understood...   (*Oratio Valedictoria*)

First, they made me an eye.
In the cold revolving stars, in the storm,
in the flying sun, in the place where water
comes out of the earth, an eye.
The eye watched; they were not alone.
They scratched its shape on stones
where the dead lay. Its rays spun out
weblike, encompassing the world;
drilled into bone, a passage, a way through.

Next, they made me a brow.
Over two staring circles, a double bow,
thick plunging curves, a look
of intense concentration. Life
with some thought behind it, an intelligence.
By now, they'd invented pots:
comfortable pregnant bellies, with twin eyes
frowning out of the clay. Sense
out of nonsense. Room to grow.

Then came the owl: that was natural.
Something alive and searching after dark —
that great dished listening face.
Soundless flight; wings a whisper of snow,
then the sudden swoop of death.

The voice of a world both fearful and beautiful
was a shuddering *hoo, hoo*. That suited me.
I flew secretly; I stunned, I wooed,
I tore apart, I saw and heard all.

And lastly, a woman born
out of sea-foam, out of flowers, or from
the head of a god — ridiculous. I'd been
too generous: the people thought too much;
they gorged on metaphors, they killed for them.
I was Athene, wise and terrible
flinging my spears, helmeted with the Moon,
crowned with stars, a woman clothed with the Sun
defending Right and Might and Truth and Freedom.

But now, little monk, by dusk
I see you kneeling on the cold flags
of your narrow cell, and your mind
is all eyes. In your heart a dark fire,
a lust. You have trusted me
and I have come: but I will not come kind
or maidenly — never forget, I am taloned,
banished from daylight, savage with desire —
but beautiful, yes my love; and I see, I see.

III
The Inner Artificer

Man labours on the surface of things; but Nature
works from within.   (*De Causa*)

The scientist's posed in a pigsty —
an awkward smile on his round foolish face —
with his creature, transgenic monster, poor pig,
blind, bloated and arthritic, a coarse slab.
That smile of hesitant triumph,
those well-scrubbed fingers touching the prone
thick body in the straw, show no remorse;
more a coy, teasing promise, an allure.

And I wonder, Bruno, what you'd think of him
that gene-magician in his white coat,
his surface-work. They still say *Mother Nature* —
meaning a woman, weak and pliable,
limited, passive, open to be explored,
discarded, raped. Mother gives more and more.

But among us, *da noi*, Nature is called
the inner artificer. And she's everywhere,
strong, steadfast: power in the womb
of matter, the spirit that shines
through things. She's a voice
heard in a room, sounding to each corner,
everywhere resonant; we can't turn from her.

And she returns us our filth, feeds us
our stored-up poison. She will not spare
the seals, or our children. Deserts balloon,
malignant. As we divide, negate,

reduce and separate, she multiplies,
joins and reshapes the world, swarms out
from the core. She is not sentimental.

This grinning alchemist plays with the parts,
blind to the whole. Like his pig
he is paralysed, stuck, sterile. He believes
in the old, flat, static Earth. He believes in Hell.

While Nature still works from her centre,
expelling galaxies, singing through every door.
Revolutionary Queen of the chromosomes,
the inner artificer. Hidden and sure.

IV
Conjuration

Why, I say, do so few understand and apprehend the internal power? ...He who sees all things, is all things.
(De Imaginum Compositione)

I draw into myself
The scarlet in this star,
The Fire that shaped the world,
All instruments of war

Heart's blood, birth-blood, stain
Of sun in a dawn sky,
Red banners blowing west
Wiping out tyranny:

I draw into myself
The green in this great wood,
The dark flood of the sea
April in blade and shoot

And breathe in liquid gold
Cold-running through my veins:
Power in the tiger's eye
Power in a storm of change

Breaking concentric spheres
Blowing from town to town
Oak-crowned, the Thunderer
Guarding the Gate of Horn

While a red-bearded King
Turns in his sleep of stone —
Ready for anything
I face this world alone.

I draw into myself
The Dragon, and the Sun;
Watchful, invincible,
My Destiny begun.

V
The Art of Memory

To understand is to speculate with images.
(De Imaginum, Signorum et Idearum Compositionae)

The sun blesses my face. I breathe
in its warm yellow strength. Stock-doves
play hollow flutes above me.
I close my eyes, assemble for a journey.

Frater Jordanus, whom you will observe
on the stone seat by the bay-tree, gazing inwards
at innumerable worlds, is our chief treasure;
a golden chestful, a dragon's hoard
of secrets. When his dark eyes turn
towards you, it's like falling into a well
that empties into night. And then there's that
slow, curved smile. Ask him:
he'll offer you jewels — he is generous,
though careful of course, as we all are,
knowing forbidden things. He stands at the brink
of a revelation, the winds of all time in his face,
his mop of hair. No, we don't yet know
what he's discovered; but he cultivates
                    our Art of Memory.

Now I build a castle on a hilltop
crowded with white towers.
In every room a thousand new spaces
that I shall fill with subtle images.
And every image wears its secret meaning:
something stupendous, unforgettable,
there, in its own place. That gives me power.

The brothers come to him, and certain books
pass from sleeve to sleeve. I think you know
what I refer to. Jordanus made our name
glorious here: the Holy Father
Himself received instruction. So you see
our problem — where to draw the line
between grace and heresy. Such brilliance,
such rainbow facets; we are all transfixed.
And this is why I point him out to you —
remember him. Sadly, he must be silenced.
A man who holds all heaven in his head
                    cannot live long.

     I know a double picture:
     the world of senses, and the world
     of image. That is my strength,
     my poetry, my secret. I have flown
     over the stars, and found no barrier,
     only more stars, more worlds.
     So listen, listen: we are all free,
     we cannot be walled in;
     not while we keep our Art of Memory,
     storehouse of truth, star-garden.
     Tremendous is the force
     of my spiritual intentions;
     empowering the message that I bear.
     Stop me, old men, if you dare.

VI
Heroic Frenzy

Is it for me to oppose the sacred order of Nature? ...I have never had a desire to become a eunuch. On the contrary, I should be ashamed to yield on that score, were it only by a hair, to any man, in order to serve Nature and God...
(De Gli Eroici Furori: preface addressed to Sir Philip Sidney)

In dawn light, Benedetta, your hair
tumbled over the pillow is darker
than resinous darkness from a cypress wood
where night still huddles; darker
than my blackest thoughts. When the sun floods
the window, you shall be brushed with copper,
ablaze with deep bronze. Here I rest my hand
on the sleeping curve of your spine, and over
the treasure of your breast, and my heart burns
with a small, secret fire. I won't forget
how I knelt to you last night, and offered homage
wordlessly, as you stood over me
shuddering in your joy. This, too,
is serving God and Nature: our splendid labour.

Waking before dawn, in my old way —
one habit I'll never lose — my morning prayer
is buried in your breathing. May it grow
inside you like a tree of white flowers
resplendent in a garden. I have come late
to this rule, this discipline, this new devotion:
forgive me, Benedetta. My life's path
is already chosen — work and loneliness.
I'm an explorer, bound for strange lands,
searching for what was lost; a buccaneer
with a price on my head; a danger. The sun
creeps up: your spread hair glows. Oh love
the choice is hard. I am a standing flame,
a bird in your hands. Hoist me high: let me go.

VII
The Journey

Any horizon, however extensive, suggests a beyond.
(De Immenso)

Setting out again, taking the road again
that leads to some new city
  Adocentyn
or, for the time, Geneva, Avignon,
Toulouse or fabled London; setting out
in the dark, on a purseful of whispers —
go there, take this, speak to that man
who bears the sign we know of — hurriedly
fastening the points of my long hose
  seeming natural to me now

abandoning these streets, these squares
these clever, spiced gardens; in my heart
  a vow to return
and a lifting spirit, a joy
taking flight, driving me on.
I shall wheel round and round
this world like a Moon, like a comet
  leaving a fiery trail

never resting until I have seen
the City of Light accomplished
and all my friends safely installed therein
gathered from here and there. With this dream
I fill spare moments waiting in the rain
for promised horses, or a weary trudge
across town after an absent-minded fool:
  all the loose, empty hours

between me and my destination. Tonight
the sky is plunged thick with stars
my wild companions, hurtling with me
to an unknown end; which doesn't matter —
only the journey matters. I breathe
clean mountain air: a vision
of Nola brushes past. *Adocentyn.*
Perfect place, place that never was
nor shall be ever, compels me.
No end, then, to the dizzy Universe,
    no end to my journeying.

VIII
Sun in Leo

...You see, then, how one simple divinity which is in all things, one fecund nature, mother and preserver of the Universe, shines forth in different subjects and takes different names... Thus we should think of Sol as being in a crocus, a daffodil, a sunflower, in the cock, in the lion...

(Lo Spaccio della Bestia Trionfante)

Brazen summer, summer burnished and bold;
the sun exalted, the sky's hot copper
scalding our eyes, a tingle on the skin

and noon like a ringing of horns
in the hills, like a hammered coin.
The roadside leaves are dusty

and glittering. Between here and the coast
acres of sunflowers turn their polished heads:
gold worshipping gold. Their hearts

are rich oil. They thrust
from cool nourishing darkness into light.
At a low whitewashed house a woman stands

framed in her doorway: by her feet
two cats, one pied, one ginger.
Her hands supporting the jambs

hold the house steady as she gazes
beyond the blazing molten faces
of the flowers, beyond the dug rock

to where the lions are. They flow and circle
on a hot yellow plain, always moving
a little nearer through the dry grass,

muscles woven under satin skin;
their eyes half-closed and gleaming.
Lions moving together, coming at last

to the streets of the city, broad paws
and heavy shoulders spilling round corners
around parked cars, stepping down alleys

staring through windows with their gold eyes.
A stink of beast. The terrible roaring.
Everyone cowering behind locked doors

except one dark child, running out to them.
The woman lifts an arm
and rubs her forehead dry. Sweat stings

the rim of her lids. The cats
stretch and roll, stretch and roll,
greedy for sun. She tells them: *It is done.*

IX
In Aegypt

That which leads us to truth... is a kind of divine igno-
rance, together with disdain of the paths we have trav-
elled, for it comes from that region towards which every
path disappears...   *(Eroici Furori)*

I have forgotten how I arrived here.
The path is swallowed up
in mist from the mountains.
So much walking after dark, always alone.

Now, suddenly, the sun has found me
in a new country; though I've seen
it in dreams. It's shaken out
below the hill in its acres

shining with inward colours. *Oh
Aegypt, Aegypt, there will remain
of thy religion only fantasy* –
we work on what has been spoiled.

But look: you too, drawing near,
coming my way, stumbling over stones.
Come close, closer; your nearness
can't hurt me now. If I could

I'd give you a word-map of this territory:
but my words have become air.
So I stand with my heart and my hands bare
waiting for you to lift your head, and see me.

And here's a secret: we've been here before
the quick way, at the gulf
of darkness, that furthest place
only found at the point of bliss, letting go

and tumbling out backwards into space
before the body kicks us into life
helpless, ecstatic, wild.
Last time, my limbs ached

for days from that journey.
So listen, and I'll tell you a mystery —
anything that's outside this unity,
soul of the world, is nothing.

We are all linked, all joined,
all travelling. You say
I can teach you something strange,
something unguessed, hidden

eyes, voices in the leaves. Oh yes,
it's all there, alive, aware:
but you know it. All those unspoken questions
unfolding warm surprising impulses

those fleeting corner-visions, unborn
poems — they are within you; all
the answers. But just ask me anything,
take my hand, follow. This is your country too.

X
The Revolving Castle

The Infinite Universe moves in circles... like the turning of
a wheel; which remains motionless in itself while all its
parts are moving.   (*Eroici Furori*)

The small spiders of spring weave webs of spun droplets
catching newly-hatched light in their filaments,
veiling their world in gauze, through which they regard
our world of crystal. Each sound, each touch
is magnified. Spiders wear their nerves
outside, in the air, their thoughts running along
the gummy, plucked strands like music.
Dark thoughts: dark, rapid music.
The trees, stone walls, wet crumbling banks, are hung
with spider-minds, revolving spiral visions
strummed in the wind. Perhaps this early sun
will bring them careless midges. The spring spiders
wait quietly for luck, one fine leg poised
to feel its tug. When it comes, it will be sudden.

*****

I too: I have been spinning:
I've spread my mind out
in coils of silk, joining
stone to star, word to tree.
I stare through its threads
at all worlds, the circles
expanding, drawing in.
It seems there are doors
between them, mostly hidden.

*****

125

What have I started? What have I set in motion?
These wheels — where will they take me? Something
is bound to happen, some shaking of the web.
I wrote my desire in wax, and transmuted it
to flame. I'm not like you, Giordano:
I'm afraid, and careful; more pliable, less fixed,
not honed to your brilliant point. You are all
swords: I'm spiderlike, labouring
in the dark, through touch, web-maker,
a bowl of water. *Spring is coming, not long now,
and then, Summer.* All our spells return on us.
Turning woman, spinning woman am I...
I can fly as high as you, for all your boasting;
and fall as hard, and make magic as lasting.

XI
Turning North

...Are we in the daylight with the light of truth rising
above our horizon, or is the day with our adversaries in
the antipodes? ...are we in the dawn that ends the night, or
in the evening of a day that is ending?
(La Cena dei Ceneri)

Wind from the Northwest, quarter of law,
a cold just wind abseiling from the mountains,
hard flurries of hail in its skirts; in its jaws

snap glowing polar crystals, a light-show
Aurora Borealis, northern dawn. We shiver
at the season's edge, at unmistakable omens;

knowing our scales are loaded, our coins spun
towards death. By an angled sun we see
the devastation around us, its causes known

or suspected, but we don't know what to do.
The people are powerless. Was it us who poisoned
the sea, who bulldozed and burned forests, who

gloried in war? We wanted to live, and for
that privilege became slaves. Our masters, our lords
control it all, would destroy all to hold power.

When we're facing the wrong way, we confuse
sunset and sunrise. Where's North? Where's day?
But now the Northern Lights, unfurling rose

and green, give us our bearings. Now we're sure
where the blame lies, and we're angry. All directions
become plain; and our ancestors move before

us with torches, Aurora Borealis, a banner flown
sky-high. We won't wait for justice:
we'll take it, we'll wield it, a thrown

hunting-spear, a sword. Remember, the lords are few
and frightened. There's danger: this could be
the last waving light before dark — what can we lose?

XII
The Divining-Bowl

Water in its proper place is not heavy, and is not a burden
to the beings that are in the depths of the sea.
                              (La Cena dei Ceneri)

My face hanging in water
is not my face, but another's
looking down at me through hooded lids
serene, stern, secretive. A New World
face, high-cheekboned, solid-mouthed:
not mine. I recoil, disturbed,
and water slides aside, rocking my head.

Somewhere deep in the house a clock
knocks its unhurried heart.
A black iron cooking-pot
sits cold on my lap for a showstone
to see by. A gypsy's crystal
might stir suspicion; mirrors
reflect too exactly. I shall use
plain, innocent water. I breathe
the surface still, and wait.

That face suspended in darkness
swings over me. I am pulled
towards it: I feel cool rising
water breath. Blood's running
to my brain, my ears are ringing,
my chest tightens. It floats,
a mask of polished wood, the face
of an old god, giving nothing
away. And it fades, as I know it should
while the water turns cloudy and dense, becomes air.
Now pictures may appear;

I know the summoning-words, though my mouth's
too stiff to shape them. I just stare
through space till my eyes sting.

Blinking, I spoil the spell; the head
reappears, the head in the well
that will not prophesy. It swims
in its element, patient, seeing the world
from its own, altered place. "Show me
my future", I whisper

but there's only smoky water,
the weight of cold iron on my knee.

XIII
Ash Wednesday

(Frankfurt, 1591)

We see how this man, as a citizen and servant of the world, a child of Father Sun and Mother Earth, because he loves the world too much, must be hated, censured, persecuted and extinguished by it. But, in the meantime, may he not be idle or badly employed while awaiting his death, his transmigration, his change...

(Spaccio: dedication to Sir Philip Sidney)

It's an old story, and I'm tired of it.
The bishop commissions a *memento mori*
in smooth Italian marble, employs a sculptor
to chisel a cadaver — stretched raw mouth,
collapsed eyeballs, neck like a throttled chicken,
empty and rotting cheeks, grotesque claw hands
over sunken belly — for the embittered bishop
to gaze upon and know the face of death.
The face of death! The plague still rages
here, in the backstreets: from crumbling walls
rats flicker in and out of sight as common
as children. On the cathedral steps a woman
sits with her dying child. Their presence offends
his reverence: he gives orders
to move them elsewhere. He'd prefer
to contemplate the ghastly dissolution
of his own flesh in marble, while the avoidable
small deaths crowd at his door.

How wretched to be poor in a town like this
full of beauties, full of books:
in a world like this, full of wonders.

When we've built our City of Light, the world
will abolish greed and hunger; yes,
it's possible, if we wish it. And death

will be respected, neither ignored nor wooed
in fascinated terror like a woman,
with careful rituals concealing fear
guilt and disgust. Death will be known
for what it is, making-new, a clean broom
sweeping the way for life, rearranging us
in shelves and corners of the universe

and I shall be dust, flying up, a billion glittering
mica-dots in the sun, one with the angels.

You will breathe me in, play in my shadows,
dip me in ink, turn my pages,
weave all my colours, fan me to flame

dance to my pattern. I shall swim
in moon-lakes of silver
watching the full earth rise.
I shall speak with the solar creatures
wading through fiery meadows: shall be
the sun too, in its splendour.
Perhaps I'll sleep in stone a million years
to be cut out like a diamond
my ashes pressed into light.

Here are my new books: figures fresh
from my mind. *On the Minimum*
(about beginnings, causes, the smallest
elements, atoms of atoms); *On Immensity*
(the Infinite Universe, the limitless,
the republics of all worlds); *On the Number One*
(about growth from tiny to huge, about Creation:
magic, faith, imagining). They're all truthful,

they'll survive me. A better monument
than this pornographic statue of despair,
these beggars at the door. It's not death I fear
the breaking-down of my tissues, the great change,
but forgetfulness. To lose
all my mind, all my labours, all
my animated pictures to age or pain —
that's the face of death I turn from,
the empty cowl. *Prega per noi
peccatori, adesso, e nell'ora...*

East wind searching my bones; a grudging Lent
starts here. God! This is a cold country.

XIV
Alchemy

We are in a state of continual transformation: fresh atoms
are continually being reincorporated in us, while others
that we received beforehand escape from us.

(De l'Infinito)

Wonderful what will come out of darkness:
stars, owl voices, sleep;

water, green shoots, birds' eggs
with their own curved darkness;

gemstones; a whole and perfect child
from my unseen recesses; delight

from behind shut lids, finding each other,
fingers and tongues made delicate by night.

Great magic's performed after sunset.

Old alchemists conjuring angels,
witches dancing spirals under the moon;

drum-shamans, their spirit journeys;
three nights in a tomb

staging a resurrection. Transformations
taking place out of ordinary sight.

Daylight gives us boundaries, fixes
everything. The world separates
into colours and chemicals, figures

and faces. Surfaces appear solid
reliable, unconfused. We can see

to operate complex machinery.
Only darkness permits mixing

of elements, stirring of essences
in secret, combing dark and bright

into new patterns while we sleep; so dawn
finds us transformed, shifted.

Star-particles link us with trees
dolphins and stones, travel through us

creating the universe. Base matter

becomes gold: in the Cauldron
of Annwn, in the crucible of mind

we're all magicians. The Hidden Stone,
Elixir of Life, eludes us; we've lost

the art of working through touch
with invisible forces: but as darkness

rises, and we grope wildly, perhaps
out of chaos the magic will come right.

XV
Triumphant Beast

I do not believe in being tied, for I am certain that all the laces and tags in the world would not suffice for that purpose.   (*Eroici Furori:* Intro)

The double-bolted door. That fool Mocenigo,
traitor, ape, he-goat, donkey, gigolo,
dog's turd, is out to betray me. He's thrown
my teachings at my face, knowledge hard won
in loneliness, given in good faith, paid for in trust
between friends — so I thought — spat on, crushed.

May his eyes rot, may his tongue swell and choke him:
may stinking weeping pustules break out on his skin...
My fists ache with hammering, my mouth's dry
with curses — it's hopeless; I'm trapped by my enemy,
and I'm the fool, the blind one. I believed
I was free, no chains could bind me, wings up my sleeves.

The moon flaps at my window: my mind's too full
for sleep. Surely truth will save me, my trained will,
my powers. It's an ill wind, perhaps, an opportunity.
But a crinkled edge of terror still licks at me,
a wicked, singing flame. I've had this dream before.
Now I wait for the night raid, the knock on the door.

XVI
The Storm

Then the Triumphant Beast is driven out; that is the vices
which predominate and oppose the divine part of us.
(Lo Spaccio della Bestia Trionfante)

May the Chains of fear
May the implacable Walls of ignorance
May the Dungeon of despair
May the Battlements of violence
Fall, fall, fall, shatter
Scatter into dust shards,
Settle into molecules of earth
Fecund, forgiving, living earth

And the Rack of nightmares
The whitehot Pincers of cruelty
The Electrodes of insane power
Be smashed forever; the Warheads
Of frantic obsession, the Poisons
Of untrammelled greed, the Daggers
Of famine be thrown aside,

Be gone, be banished from us
For all time, the Jackboots of tyranny
The Noose of superstition, the Bludgeon
Of contempt, the Laboratory
Of arrogance, the Parliament of lies.
May they be powerless, futile, flicker-out
Into original darkness, be unmade,
Dissolved, defused, neutered,
Become soil and trees again, become rain.

Thunder cracks and growls its warning. A yellow light
sweats from mean slots of sky beyond the grille.
Searing flash: an explosion of heaven, a rupture
of stretched air; and out there the rain starts
in loud, thick drops, in hurrying muttering thousands,
nailing dust to earth, hammering into the ground,
spurting in noisy channels, chiming off metal,
smoking off roofs and cobbles, pumping up sound.
Each drop is a phial of scent breaking, releasing
essence of leafwater and stone, tree rubbings,
exhalations of flowers, a sea-tang. Even here, the smell
of crushed mountain herbs. My heart lifts and grows
like a shoot splitting open, drinking cloud water
in thankful, long gulps. Thunder trembles
in the walls, and I am suddenly lightened
released, restored, returned to my good senses.
There's revolution in heaven, the stars are changing.

May the Lion of courage
May the Dragon of knowledge
May the Daystar of cherished hopes
May the Moon of love
Shine, shine on us, may we turn
Our faces up to theirs:

The Country of healing dreams
(only found at the point of bliss)
The Ocean of compassion
The Mountain of inner power
(and the white track up to the summer pasture)
Be there for us, O may we walk there
in freedom, in balance, in simplicity;
And may the Cauldron of plenty
Brim over, feed the children:

May we put on justice, our Clothes
Of brilliant colours, worn openly
Danced in; may we understand
This living world, this Universe, all
Worlds, each other, respect
Life, respect Earth, our wayward
Selves; and gathering the Flowers
Of humility — not in guilt now
But innocence — run back, back to our old
Home, the forgotten land, the Garden.

Lightning arrows down, sings in the gutters, flares
to find me in my cell, rekindles my centre.
Then the thunderstorm rolls away, rolls into the hills.

*****

*"Let this not trouble you, Momus," said Isis, "since fate
has ordained a vicissitude of darkness and light."*

*"But the worst of it is," said Momus, "that they hold it
for certain that they are in the light..."*

XVII
Cosmology

The soul is not in the body: the body is in the soul. It is steeped in the soul like a net in the sea.

(Eroici Furori)

Stars on this high dizzy night
now my eyes are washed dark
of artificial indoor light, shine
down, down, into the measureless reaches
of the sky's ocean, layers deep
skimming aside from my hand
plunged among them. I know
without benefit of telescopic sight

the universe is not exploding out
from its centre like a bomb, a point
of ignition. The centre's everywhere,
and everywhere's expanding, not
ripping apart but sailing out
on a grand exhalation, outbreath
of life, which moves the waters
above and below, stirs weathers

and galaxies, clouds and sap,
pumping the blood around.
In this outbreath we live:
float, swim, soar, fall,
journey out and return, increase
and sparkle. After a time
there'll be a breathing-in
contraction to density, Destiny

and then out again, life again.
No, I'll not be part of a detonation,
some celestial terrorist act.
I'd rather be part of an infinite
animal, microbe of dragon-breath —
or a droplet of stupendous, thundering wave
breaking on the sands of eternity
poured out, poured out into the sky.

An image of hope displayed: a young woman rising
from the foam of the sea, who on reaching the shore
wipes off the humour of the sea with her palms....
and another image: a woman kneeling naked
in starlight by a gleaming pool, and with vessels
in either hand, from which she pours water
onto the parched land, and into the pool.

I swim in nurturing liquid, a child
in the womb of matter. The holy well
uncoils its rivers in me, its threads of light.
A taste of stone in the water, of rock,
the bones of earth. Closing my eyes, I see it,
taste, feel it; and I'm young again
and in Nola, filling stone jars with my mother
who said, Don't spill a drop, it's rare
and precious, there are stars asleep in it;
it holds their powerful rays. Dissolved
in dew, their distant fires, shaping my days.

XVIII
The Voyager

Wisdom is set in our spirit, seated on the poop of our soul, holding the tiller of the ship which it steers across the tempestuous sea of the century.
(Oratio Valedictoria)

I'm your silver, I'm your guide in the night, your dancer,
your voyager sailing the storm, your adventurer
feathered strokes dipping waterskin, a rainbow dazzle
flung out on the tips of my wings, the whisperer
in your inner ear, your deceiver, impossible sweet
changing-faced lover, your infinitely wild
passionate unrestrained your divine possessor
who rises and shines above time and reflects
the universe in your mind, the torch that shows
all your coloured images; I'm a dolphin-rider
dragging you into the sea, strange shapes in the water
rising to meet, dissolving you bone from bone, a
bitter solution, drinking you in; I'm your muse
I'm your madness, your loneliness, wanting you only
for me to play my rays on, mirror me in your eyes,
surprise and creep up behind, to find you out,
turn you round about and devour you, feed you
to the wolves, chop and change you, rearrange
your careful thoughts, circles of memory unspun
flung overboard and drowned; but plunge deep
in me, they'll be found whole and new, restored
if you trust me: I'm your last hope, your saviour
healer and teacher, your light when all lights
go out, your mariner. So follow me, take my hand,
let me sidle into your dreams, there's no need to be
afraid, I'm only the shadow, pure moonlight, look
through me and see the sun rise, the voyage made.

XIX
Solstice

The Sun must move, if it is a fire, because Fire is the most
mobile of the elements. When we prevent flames from
rising, when we imprison them in the bowels of the
furnace, they twist impatiently about themselves.

(La Cena dei Ceneri)

Hot yellow moon rose
last night, transformed
into sun, deep gold
over intense black rustling
leaves breathing stored
green scent of long day;
so all night the sky
shone, there was no night:
the triumph of light

renewed, Summer, most fiercely
hoped-for, called up
out of strength in the cold
months, with force,
with images of lions.
Sun in glory, at
zenith, convulsed with fire;
astronomers predict
magnetic surges, solar storms,
electrical disruption, flares
leaping millions of miles.

When the transformation
comes, it will be sudden
gold forming in the crucible.

The flame erupts, it must
move, must burn, no
turning-back seasons
scuttling down nocturnal
holes; its rays penetrate
to the core of matter,
change everything. We've
reason to hope: after four
hundred mechanistic years
of dispiriting gloom

the sun breaks through,
revealing a world alive
and us at the chasm's brink
shocked, lost, amazed.

Today's warm to touch,
ripens grass, blackcurrants,
my yeasty skin. Bees
cluster and dip dark heads
into purple sage. The air
seethes, stirred by the sun.
We breathe in its ferment
it moves us from the inside;
it's a secret
process, most magical.
The world must turn
to receive dawn, to receive
Summer; and we
are the world waking up

the trees reborn
over their charred stumps
the clean seas rising.

XX
Field of Flowers

Time takes everything and gives everything. All things change. Nothing is destroyed forever. *(Candelaio)*

Perhaps you are more afraid in passing this sentence than I am in hearing it. (G. Bruno to his judges: from the *Summary* of his trial.)

It's winter out there, in the world,
in the old Field of Flowers
paved with dead stones, dusted with corpse
salts and gritty leavings, smoke-blown and sour.

Waiting for dawn, for the last
time, on my knees in the listening
dark (that has always frightened me, who
was born to see the sun) I can't stop shivering

and thinking of fire. It's my way
out of cold, out of winter, infernal
circles of this prison, which I have chosen:
to blaze like a torch, escape in a churning

column of smoke over the domes and spires
and towers and pinnacles of Rome
to be blown, blown away. Calcination,
rendering down to ash, to scorched crumbs,
                                greasy foam:

the first degree of transformation. Out there
in the wind, in the public eye
of morning, shaven and bound and given
to the flames, I shall struggle and choke and die.

It's winter, but spring is coming,
not long now; and then — I forget:
it's too dark, the flowers are blotted-out.
Ripples of memory dwindle behind my shut

lids; statues, seals, hieroglyphs, gods
and graces falling away. I turn
like a moth in the vast night of unknowing
drawn by one light, one lovely flame that will burn

me up: one lust, one lunacy. Let me
go — I'm engulfed in her dazzling wings
taken in to the hammering heart of fire, its secrets.
From a cypress beyond the gates, dawn preens and sings.

XXI
The Dance

There is a continual rising and falling through the chain
of the elements... By connecting higher with lower, you
have one beautiful animal, the World.

(De Umbris Idearum)

1

Press your ear to the ground. Hear
buzzing through soil and nerve, the long
slow life of the Earth, its rage
and weariness. Don't be surprised:
you always knew it was so, that Earth
stored lives, deaths, memories
in its teeming cells. The thoughts of the Earth
are my thoughts. You are right to be afraid.

2

If you fly too close to the sun you'll burn;
your wings will melt, you'll fall
and the sea will swallow you. Too much light
sends you insane: the only remedy
is to hang by a foot in the dusk
with your nose to Earth, learn stillness
at the heart of the dance, the bent-
legged Kathakali posture that commands
attention. Bruno, you soared, you flew
crazy rejoicing lover of the world, and the world
upset, upended you. Now through closed
eyes, through dreams, your night-fears
vanished, through poems, through touch
in darkness you feel your way back, lit only
fitfully by the moon. Now your voice is
the voice of Earth, which we strain to hear.

3

Spinning translucent jewel
falling back into night,
point of light in the caverns
of fire-gems, with its life-blue
its spiral of winds:
we don't surmise, we know
we belong to a star, a famous
luminary. We are the Heavens
the Firmament, the angelic realm
glimpsed from great airless spaces;
here is Paradise, the Garden,
our only home, the shining
City, Adocentyn in all colours
and images, the World
that was always there but mostly
invisible, turning and changing
changing us, whether we will
or no: and inside it's burning.

4

Dancing the wild atomic reel
The Old Wheels of the World, a tune
Taught us, it's said, by the fairies —

Shiva's dance in his ring of flames —
Life came through the cosmic gates
Weaving its nets, its sidesteps

Its chancy patterns. Science rests
On illusions, reflections, shadows
Of lifting footsteps, echoes of half

Heard music. Caught in the dance
We can't stop to analyse, but must
Learn to love dancing, moved by inner

Drumming, swung rhythms begun
By our ancient Mother the Sea.
At the hub of her web, the Spider also

Dances, draws cords from her body, circles
Outwards then winds them in
To the spool of herself, the World

Pulled out, drawn back by those threads
Which we all spin, webwork of memory
And Love. In the well, the womb-waters

Our future multiplies, particles of soul
Dance through the elements, and I take
The hands of all my loves, and we begin.

Now I understand, I understand everything.

Notes on the Poems

The Tree Calendar

ROWAN
The Feast Day of Bride, or Brigid, (February 1st) occurs during
the Rowan month. The quotation at the beginning of the poem is
from A. Carmichael's *Carmina Gaedelica*.

ASH
The Ash is the World Tree of Norse mythology, from which
Odin hung to gain knowledge of the Runes. Beneath it sit the
three Norns (Fates), eternally spinning the webs of Wyrd that
govern our lives.

ALDER
The story referred to is the legend of Taliesin, miraculous child
and poet/prophet.
Brân is Welsh for crow or raven, and the name of the British god
of eloquence, whose "head" is buried on Tower Hill in London.
The Alder was sacred to him.
green as thieves... Alder flowers yield a green dye, once used to
camouflage the clothes of forest dwellers and outlaws.

HOLLY
The Festival of Lammas or Lughnasadh (August 1st) occurs
during the Holly month. At this season, many early agrarian
cultures sacrificed a young man, who represented the powers of
plant growth. His blood was sprinkled on the fields and his flesh
was ritually eaten. He was reborn at the Winter Solstice, when
we decorate our houses with Holly.

HAZEL
In Celtic myth, the Well at the World's End is the source of all
wisdom and knowledge. Hazel trees grow over it and drop their
nuts into the water. The Salmon of wisdom swims in the pool
and eats the magical nuts.

IVY

The Nine Kings of the North Pole descend... This line is the title of a
Chinese festival which occurs at this season.
splitting apart... Several of the words and images in this poem are
inspired by one of the oracular Chinese hexagrams of the
I-Ching; the hexagram *Po* (Splitting Apart) which is linked to the
late autumn.

ELDER

Huldre Folk... These are dangerous woodland beings, who are de-
ceptively beautiful until they turn their backs, which are said to
be hollow. They are particularly associated with Elder trees.
Old Mother...etc. This is an old East Anglian spell, to be said in the
unlucky event of cutting an Elder tree. A version of it, with a
Scandinavian equivalent, is given in Katherine Brigg's *The Hidden
People.*

CANDLEMAS

The Christian feast of Candlemas (February 2nd) occurs during
the Celtic festivals of Imbolc or Brigid/Bride. Both are purifica-
tion festivals celebrating the return of light to the earth in late
winter. My father died in the early hours of February 2nd 1981.

THE SONG OF BLODEUWEDD ON MAY MORNING

With calmness, with care/with breastmilk, with dew... These words
are from the ecstatic trance-utterances of Maria Sabina, Mazatec
Indian shaman. Some other phrases in the poem are also inspired
by her words.
The story of Blodeuwedd can be read in the tale of Math Son of
Mathonwy from *The Mabinogion.* In this poem she binds her lover
Gronw to her with a spell.

BODHRÁN

A Bodhrán is an Irish frame-drum, of a type common in many
other cultures. It is identical with the shaman drum of all
Northern peoples. Nowadays it is used extensively in traditional
folk music, and is played mainly by men; once it was a women's
instrument, and was also used for winnowing grain. It used to be
beaten with a bone, but is now played with a wooden beater.

WINTER SOLSTICE
Gawain is a reference to the mediaeval poem *Sir Gawain and the Green Knight*. Gawain's journey to find the Green Chapel took place at the Winter Solstice.

HUNTING THE WREN
This custom, once widespread in the British Isles, involved young men killing a wren on St Stephen's Day (Boxing Day), putting the wren into a decorated box, and carrying it from house to house in return for pennies. The traditional song accompanying this custom is usually known as *The Cutty Wren* One version begins:

"O where are you going?" says Milder to Molder.
"We're hunting the wren" says Jackie the Can.
"We're hunting the wren" says Johnnie Red Nose.
"We're hunting the wren" says everyone.

Book of Shadows

TWO RIVERS

THE SEALWIFE
There is a story from Scotland about a fisherman who takes a wife from among the seal people. He watches them dance by moonlight, and steals one of their sealskins and hides it in the rocks. When dawn approaches, the sealfolk hurry back into their sealskins and return to the sea, except for one young woman whose skin it is that was stolen. Regretfully, her people leave her on the shore, and the fisherman carries her off to live with him. She becomes his wife and bears him several children, but she always longs to return to her own people. One day, the children come running in from the beach. One of them has something he has found in the rocks: her old sealskin. She pulls it on, says a sorrowful farewell to her children, and swims out to sea. It is said that she sometimes returned to speak with them from the safety of a rock a little way from the shore; but she never set foot on land again.

BREAKFAST WITH THE POETS
The city of Almería in South-eastern Spain was the centre of an
ancient Moorish kingdom. In its heyday in the 11th century AD it
was famous throughout Europe as an important port for trade
with North Africa, and was noted for its astoundingly beautiful
weaving; and also for its poets. It was one of the last cities in
Spain to fall to the Catholics, and the only one to have been
shelled by the Nazis. Since the Catholic Reconquest in the 15th
century Almería has been in a slow decline, and only now with
tourism steadily encroaching eastward from the Costa del Sol is
the city again beginning to expand. Almería is my maternal
grandfather's city: he was born in the village of Oanes in the
Alpujarra mountains to the north-west, in the fertile valley of the
river Andarax (now decimated by drought).

Almería is still noted for its poets, and while visiting with my
family I attended a poetry reading at dawn in the Moorish
fortress, the Alcazaba above the town. The reading included
Moorish music and dance, and a *desayuno* of herb tea, fruit and
'Moorish' cakes afterwards. The event was to celebrate a famous
Almerían poet: Al-Mutasim Ibn Sumadih, king of Almería in the
late 11th century. Contemporary poets read from his work in
Spanish, and also from their own work.
...*See, I have laid...* This is my translation of an extract from one of
Mutasim's poems, translated into Spanish by Amelina Ramon
Guerrero, Professor of Arabic Studies at the University of
Granada.

BOOK OF SHADOWS

Giordano Bruno was born in Nola, southern Italy in 1548 and
was burnt at the stake in Rome in 1600. He became famous in his
early twenties, while still in his monastery in Naples, as an out-
standing practitioner of the *Ars Memoriae* or Art of Memory. This
was an ancient and complex mnemoic system, in which one
imagined a room and peopled it with the facts one wished to re-
member in the form of symbolic objects around the room. So
when you wanted to recall a specific fact, you merely entered
your imaginary room, remembering on which chair or in which
alcove or on which windowsill that fact was perched, and there it
was waiting for you, in whatever graphic and stunning form you

had invested it. The memory room could be expanded as need arose, to become a cathedral or palace or memory theatre of whatever subtle or intricate design you chose, provided it was logical, and thereby easily committed to memory. It is said of Bruno that he soon ran out of places to house all the things he wished to remember (because he wished to remember all the knowledge of the world). So he asked his superiors if it was permissible to travel in his imagination beyond the Earth and its spheres to the stars and the heavens. The answer was no; it was not permissible: but he did so anyway, in the quest for other worlds in which to place his thoughts. And that is how he began his dangerous speculations on astronomy and the true nature of the Universe. Well, it makes a good story.

Bruno was a prolific writer during his short career, and many of his writings are in the form of poetry. He spent a couple of years in England (1583-6) and became a well-known figure at the court of Elizabeth I. During his English exile he wrote several of his most interesting works, including his great poetic treatise *De Gli Eroici Furori* (On Heroic Frenzy) which he dedicated to his good friend Sir Philip Sidney. Both Bruno and Sidney had close links with Welsh magician Dr. John Dee and his circle. Bruno had a Scottish disciple called Dicson who did a lot to popularise his philosophy in Britain. There is evidence, too, that Shakespeare knew of Bruno and his teachings and may have been influenced by them (see F. Yates: *Giordano Bruno and the Hermetic Tradition,* ch. XIX). In fact, the name of Giordano Bruno was notorious throughout Europe. He continued to be an important influence on non-Establishment thought until about the middle of the 17th century, when the new scientific rationalism finally triumphed.

The main thrust of his philosophy, which had its roots in the ancient world and its branches in the new learning of the Renaissance, was (briefly) this:

—That Nature is alive, and that all life is animated from within, not from any outer force. Matter and Spirit are indivisible, and Matter is divine.

— All life-forms are inter-related and formed from the same basic ingredients; therefore we should respect all forms of life.

— That the Universe is infinite, and contains innumerable worlds. (He found the vast scale of the Universe joyful and heartening rather than fearful and depressing.) That there are also infinite possibilities for change in the world.

— The supreme importance of the Poet in society (on a par with the Magus), as someone able to *change* and *shape* events as well as to reflect and comment on them.

— The need to turn to alternative, non-Christian beliefs and cultures for the creative wisdom to balance our dominant world-view.

— The possibility of a better, juster society, and our duty to strive to improve social justice.

—Sexual love, religious ecstasy, poetic inspiration and intellectual vision are all expressions of one divine 'heroic frenzy', which is the creative urge that gives birth to the Universe.

For these beliefs, and for his avowed intentions to replace the Christianity of those times with a new religion based on creative magic, Bruno was burnt to death on the Campo de Fiori in Rome after eight years' imprisonment in the dungeons of the Inquisition.

Bruno was brought up in Aristotle's universe of fixed elements and starry spheres, with Heaven above and beyond it all, and Hell somewhere deep in the Earth — that lowliest object furthest removed from God. His realisation — however he came by it — that the vision was false, that the Earth is no more at the centre than anywhere else is, that the rigid circles of existence culminating in Heaven were an illusion, the Universe in fact being infinitely vast with innumerable stars and planets; that realisation gave him an exhilarating sense of release that we find hard to imagine nowadays. Perhaps it was all too much for him. Perhaps it sent him mad: he certainly suffered from some strange delusions (The Pope would listen to his ideas and welcome them... Single-handedly, the Nolan would change the world...). But it was a creative madness all the same; the madness of a poet. It is this poet's excitement that spills out into his writing, making it more than philosophy or even mere magical esoterics. Without the poetic fire, the 'Heroic

Frenzy', it would be obscure and unreadable today. Yet Bruno's story and his strange ideas continue to capture our imaginations, those of us who are rebels at heart, poets at heart.

There is another important strand in these poems, as important (so it's turned out) as Giordano Bruno himself, though I confess that wasn't my original intention.

I needed a structure to work to, one that suited the general atmosphere of Bruno's ideas and times, which would be relevant to my own experience too. So I chose the Tarot, a collection of symbols in pictorial form, familiar to me and surely familiar to Bruno as well. A common point of reference, perhaps. These days the cards are used chiefly for fortune telling, but they have other uses too. I like to look at the pictures and think about what they symbolise, treat them as visual metaphors, rich sources of imagery.

Each poem in the sequence has a relationship to one of the 22 cards of the Major Trumps of the Tarot. The relationship varies from tenuous (e.g. *The Inner Artificer*) to fairly direct (*Cosmology*). The poems are numbered according to the usual numbering of the Tarot Trumps, from 0 to 21, and they match the usual order of the cards.

I first became interested in Bruno through reading a novel: a strange, rich novel by the American author John Crowley, called *Little, Big*. His next novel, *Aegypt*, features Bruno much more directly, through the device of a book within a book (one of the many books within that book). Because of the glimpses in Crowley's books of something mysterious and compelling, I wanted to know more, and I found scholarly works that made my head spin. But I felt I was on the edge of discovering, or rediscovering, something quite simple and familiar. So I wanted to go further in, and as a poet, it seemed to me that the way in was through poetry; and Bruno was a poet too. And that is how these poems began.

Tarot Correspondences

0	THE FOOL	(Nola)
I	THE MAGICIAN	(Book of Shadows)
II	THE HIGH PRIESTESS	(Athene)
III	THE EMPRESS	(The Inner Artificer)
IV	THE EMPEROR	(Conjuration)
V	THE HIEROPHANT/POPE	(The Art of Memory)
VI	THE LOVERS	(Heroic Frenzy)
VII	THE CHARIOT	(The Journey)
VIII	STRENGTH	(Sun In Leo)
IX	THE HERMIT	(In Aegypt)
X	THE WHEEL OF FORTUNE	(The Revolving Castle)
XI	JUSTICE	(Turning North)
XII	THE HANGED MAN	(The Divining-Bowl)
XIII	DEATH	(Ash Wednesday)
XIV	TEMPERANCE	(Alchemy)
XV	THE DEVIL	(Triumphant Beast)
XVI	THE TOWER	(The Storm)
XVII	THE STAR	(Cosmology)
XVIII	THE MOON	(The Voyager)
XIX	THE SUN	(Solstice)
XX	JUDGEMENT	(Field of Flowers)
XXI	THE WORLD	(The Dance)

NOLA
Nola was Bruno's birthplace, a town in the Campagna of
Southern Italy, within sight of Mt. Vesuvius.
our green mountain: Monte Cicala, Nola's local hill.
bee-swarms in the earth: this alludes to the phenomenon called the
Hummadruz, of unknown origin, that is occasionally experienced
on hot windless days, especially on hilltops or around ancient
sites.

BOOK OF SHADOWS
Modern occultists often refer to their personal books of ritual or
magical diaries as their *Book of Shadows*. Most are unaware that
the term was popularised by the success of Bruno's first pub-
lished work *De Umbris Idearum* (On the Shadows of Ideas), a

treatise on magical conjuration and astrology. This, together with Cornelius Agrippa's *Occult Philosophy*, was secretly read by many would-be conjurers, at great danger to themselves, as possession of these books was considered proof of diabolical heresy. As late as the 19th century in Brittany, many country folk kept a book of spells, usually chained and padlocked, known as an *Agrippa*. It was thought dangerous for anyone other than the village priest to make use of an *Agrippa* (see Derek Bryce: *The Celtic Legend of the Beyond*). In other parts of France and in England such spell-books were sometimes known as a *Book of Shadows*.

The image of a broken mirror in the first stanza comes from *Lamps of the Thirty Statues*. In the poems that follow, I have occasionally borrowed from Bruno's prolific and often startling imagery.

ATHENE
In the opening quotation (from a farewell speech given at the University of Wittenburg) Bruno is referring to Minerva the Goddess of Wisdom (Athene in Greece), whose emblem was an owl. The owl motif can be traced back to prehistoric 'Eye Goddess' representations.

THE INNER ARTIFICER
This poem arose from a photograph of a transgenic pig developed by genetic scientists at the US Dept. of Agriculture, Beltsville, Maryland. The pig had been implanted with human growth gene. It grew quickly to a huge size, but was blind, excessively hairy, sterile and crippled with arthritis.
The monster's creators considered Pig 6707 a great scientific advance. The poem's title is from a statement of Bruno's concerning Nature as the creative power of the Universe: *Da noi si chiama artifice interna*. This phrase is translated at the beginning of stanza 3. Every other statement in that stanza is also taken directly from Bruno.

THE JOURNEY
Adocentyn was first described in a mediaeval Spanish/Arabic book of magic called *Picatrix* (a book of terrifying reputation), as a marvellous city built by Hermes Trismegistus, the mythical founder of alchemy and magical lore. Adocentyn was situated

"in the east of Egypt" and was twelve miles long, and contained speaking statues and a great tree "which bore the fruit of all generation". It also contained a tower with a lighthouse rotating in seven colours, one for each day of the week. Images placed around the city walls helped to make the inhabitants virtuous and to protect them from harm. Many Renaissance philosophers were inspired by Adocentyn to propose similar Utopian cities or states, based on harnessing beneficial supernatural forces (see F. Yates: *Giordano Bruno and the Hermetic Tradition*).

SUN IN LEO
A talismanic poem, summoning the virtue of Strength or Fortitude. The tarot card *Strength* generally depicts a woman with a lion in a desert landscape. Its equivalent among the suit cards, The Queen of Wands, shows an enthroned woman surrounded by sunflowers with cats at her feet.

IN AEGYPT
To understand exactly what I mean by the term "Aegypt" (as opposed to Egypt), you will have to read John Crowley's novel of that title. In the meantime, Crowley's suggestion is that there were two "Egypts" in the ancient world: the historical Egypt of the Pharaohs, and another Egypt, a country of the imagination, whose borders may, or may not, have touched the "real" Egypt — a mysterious region from which came all magical arts and skills, a shadow country of great wisdom that was in some ways like Egypt but "not Egypt, not Egypt at all... but Aegypt" (John Crowley: *Aegypt*, pp. 99-102). The real Egypt we now know to have been a fairly barbarous place, with a tyrannical state based on slavery and a grotesque, deathbound religion, materialistic and superstitious. Yet throughout the Middle Ages and even up to the present day, Egypt has been revered as the source of great civilisation and arcane wisdom, a magnet for romantic imaginings. Egypt has been confused with Aegypt: and Aegypt has fallen, with her secret doctrines, her harmonious religion of life (not death), her wise women and men, all barely more than a legend, fragmented and scattered.

For the alchemists and hermetic philosophers such as Bruno, some of the old Tale and teachings of Aegypt were preserved in a collection of writings, the *Corpus Hermeticum*, once thought to be older than Moses, but discovered in the 17th century to date from the 2nd century AD. These mysterious and beautiful writings from the last years of Paganism were an inspiration to Bruno: he continually quotes from them or alludes to them. It was his belief that Aegypt could be restored and its truths revealed, its "religion of the world" returned to, to the betterment of human society. That was his mission, his Great Work, to be accomplished through magic and poetry.

"O Aegypt, Aegypt": from the *Corpus Hermeticum*; the "Lament for the Egyptian Religion".

In my poem, Aegypt is a region of dreams and of ecstasy, the place where everything becomes clearly understood. We help each other to discover it, through sharing knowledge, and also through sexual passion, the sharing of delight. The idea being that Aegypt is an integral part of each of us, our hidden potential, our powers to transform.

THE REVOLVING CASTLE
The title is a translation of *Caer Sidi*, the castle of the Celtic Goddess Arianrhod, ruler of the turning heavens (and therefore of Fate). One of her emblems was the Spider. Arianrhod means "Silver Wheel", another image of the constellations.

TURNING NORTH
Quarter of law... according to Native American tradition, each compass direction has a symbolic meaning or "medicine" — hence the "Medicine Wheel". In the Medicine Wheel the North West is the direction of Law, meaning natural law, and the morality of nature that says "as you sow, so shall you reap", the Law of Returns. The restoration of *law* (a society based on natural justice) was a recurring theme of Bruno's.

Remember, the lords are few... here is a nod, a respectful and admiring nod, in the direction of Ursula K. Le Guin's *City of Illusions*.

ASH WEDNESDAY
"*Prega per noi/peccatori*": from the Italian *Hail Mary* — "pray for us sinners, now, and at the hour (of our death)".

TRIUMPHANT BEAST
Zuan Mocenigo, a wealthy Venetian, invited Bruno to his house
in 1592, to learn from him the secrets of the Art of Memory. After
Bruno had stayed with him for about two months, Mocenigo be-
came alarmed at the extent of the Nolan's heresies, and refused
to allow him to return to Germany. He locked Bruno in his room
and denounced him to the Inquisition, who dragged him from
his bed in the early hours of May 26th 1592. As Frances Yates ob-
serves: "On that day began for Bruno eight years of imprison-
ment ending in death".

THE STORM
The incantatory sections are inspired by Bruno's extraordinary
conjuration for "the Reform of the Heavens" in *Lo Spaccio della
Bestia Trionfante* (The Expulsion of the Triumphant Beast).
Let this not trouble you, Momus... this snatch of dialogue is also
from *Spaccio*.

SOLSTICE
The Sun must move... Bruno believed, with Copernicus, that the
Earth and other planets moved round the Sun. But his specula-
tions went way beyond Copernicus, some of them fantastically
wild (such as assuming intelligent lifeforms on every heavenly
body, including the Sun), and some surprisingly accurate (such
as his explanation for the motions of the Earth and the fluctua-
tion of seasons). He thought the Sun must turn on its axis *because
it is a fire, and Fire is mobile*; he thought the Earth "wobbled" on its
axis, producing the seasons *because the Earth in its wisdom wanted
to bring the benefits of sunlight to all its parts* — this shows how
very differently his mind worked from that of conventional
astronomers.

FIELD OF FLOWERS
Bruno was burnt alive in the Campo de Fiori in Rome on
February 17th 1600. Several witnesses testified to his death.
This Roman square was the site of countless horrible executions.
Strangely enough, while I was writing these poems I noticed a
car advertisement in one of the Sunday colour supplements that
was set in the Campo de Fiori. On the damp cobbles of the

square was a bright red car, and under the square's name was a smart *gelateria* offering Visa facilities. How times have changed!

THE DANCE
The thoughts of the Earth... from a Navajo Indian chant

It is lovely indeed, it is lovely indeed:
I, I am the spirit within the Earth.
The feet of the Earth are my feet;
The legs of the Earth are my legs;
The strength of the Earth is my strength;
The voice of the Earth is my voice;
The thoughts of the Earth are my thoughts;
The feather of the Earth is my feather.
All that belongs to the Earth belongs to me;
All that surrounds the Earth surrounds me;
For I, I am the sacred words of the Earth:
It is lovely indeed, it is lovely indeed.

I belong to a star, a famous luminary... G. Bruno: *De Immenso IV.*
The Old Wheels of the World is the title of an Irish reel, one of the many traditional tunes reputed to have come to humankind from the fairies.